getting district
results

A Case Study in
Implementing
PLCs at Work™

Nicholas Jay Myers

Foreword by Richard DuFour and Rebecca DuFour

Solution Tree | Press

a division of

Solution Tree

555 North Morton Street
Bloomington, IN 47404

800.733.6786 (toll free) / 812.336.7700
FAX: 812.336.7790

email: info@solution-tree.com
solution-tree.com

Printed in the United States of America

16 15 14 13 12   1 2 3 4 5

Library of Congress Cataloging-in-Publication Data

Myers, Nicholas Jay.
  Getting district results : a case study in implementing PLCS at work / Nicholas Jay Myers.
      p. cm.
  ISBN 978-1-936764-32-7 (perfect bound : alk. paper) -- ISBN 978-1-936764-33-4 (library edition : alk. paper)
  1. School improvement programs--Illinois--Schaumburg (Township)--Case studies. 2. Professional learning communities--Illinois--Schaumburg (Township)--Case studies. 3. Schaumburg Township School District 54 (Ill.)--Case studies. I. Title.
  LB2822.83.I3M94 2012
  371.2'07097737731
                          2012009241

Solution Tree
Jeffrey C. Jones, CEO
Edmund M. Ackerman, President

Solution Tree Press
President: Douglas M. Rife
Publisher: Robert D. Clouse
Vice President of Production: Gretchen Knapp
Managing Production Editor: Caroline Wise
Senior Production Editor: Suzanne Kraszewski
Copy Editor: Rachel Rosolina
Proofreader: Ashante Thomas
Text Designer: Jenn Taylor
Cover Designer: Rian Anderson

acknowledgments

This book is written in dedication to and recognition of the hard work of Schaumburg Township School District 54's students, staff, parents, community volunteers, and board of education. Special thanks must be expressed to Rick and Becky DuFour for their tireless commitment to empowering educators with systematic approaches proven to improve learning outcomes for students. Schaumburg's successes are the result of the application of Rick and Becky's work—our students are the beneficiaries of your vision for schools.

Additionally, I would like to express my gratitude to four key mentors who impacted my vision and leadership in the field of education in profound ways: I was blessed at a very young age to work as a student teacher with Toby Boss at Waverly High School. Toby taught me how to connect with students, honor and respect instructional time, and make learning relevant and meaningful for all children. This early experience as a student teacher was critical to my future successes in the field. Thank you for preparing me for the journey, Toby.

I was equally fortunate to work for and with Bob Lipinski during my first teaching and administrative positions. Bob impressed upon me how important passion, tenacity, attention to detail, and work ethic are in all that we do as school leaders. My early experiences in teaching and administration were shaped by Bob's belief in teamwork and in framing all decisions around working in the best interest of students. Thanks for strengthening me, Bob.

In my first principalship, I replaced the man I had served as an assistant principal for during the previous two school years. John Sanders broadened my understanding of educational leadership and had a tremendous impact on my communication style. I learned a great deal about balancing the stresses of home and work, and finding fulfillment in both, from John. Thank you for broadening my perspective, John.

Finally, I have had the true privilege of working for and with Ed Rafferty for the past eight years as a principal and now as assistant superintendent. Under Ed's mentorship, I have learned how to focus efforts, avoid complacency, and never waiver from making difficult decisions that are ultimately in the best interest of students. I've learned how to laugh and truly enjoy the people and challenges that confront us each day in our field. Thank you for your continual impact, Ed.

I would also like to thank my family for all of their support throughout the years. My parents, who supported me in my decision to enter the field of education and have always made time to listen when I needed to share career- and home-related stresses, challenges, and successes, provided me with the foundation I needed to be successful. Thank you for equipping me, Mom and Dad.

Most important, my wife Adrianne has been a constant source of support, strength, and love as we have moved through many different career stages and the challenges associated with each. She is my greatest supporter, thoughtful critic, honest sounding board, and best friend. Thank you for giving me a great life, Adrianne.

Visit **go.solution-tree.com/plcbooks** for links to materials related to this book.

---

table of contents

about the author

 **Nicholas Jay Myers, EdD,** is assistant superintendent for student learning in Schaumburg Township School District 54, the largest elementary school district in Illinois. He supports the implementation of the professional learning community model in the twenty-seven diverse elementary and junior high schools in the district. Dr. Myers is former principal of Anne Fox School in Hanover Park, Illinois, a targeted assistance Title I school with an exceptionally diverse student population. As a result of its transformation into a PLC, Fox experienced dramatic improvement in student achievement.

During Dr. Myers' tenure, Fox moved from 68 percent of students meeting or exceeding state academic standards in 2005 to more than 95 percent in 2009. The school's story of academic resurgence has been documented in the *Chicago Tribune, Daily Herald,* and the *Illinois Alumni* magazine. Fox is included as a model PLC on the allthingsPLC.com website and was referenced in Richard DuFour and Robert Marzano's 2011 book *Leaders of Learning.* Fox received the 2007 and 2008 Academic Improvement Award from the Illinois State Board of Education for significant gains in academic achievement. For his leadership, Dr. Myers received a Those Who Excel Award from the Illinois State Board of Education. His article "Block Scheduling That Gets Results" was featured in the November/December 2008 edition of *Principal* magazine and his co-authored article "Moving Up From Mediocre" was featured in the January 2012 edition of *School Administrator.*

Dr. Myers earned a bachelor's degree in education at the University of Nebraska, a master's degree in administration from Northern Illinois University, and a doctorate in educational leadership and organizational change from Roosevelt University.

To book Dr. Myers for professional development, contact pd@solution-tree.com.

foreword

BY **Richard DuFour and Rebecca DuFour,**
Education Authors and Consultants

Let us begin with a story: A team of engineers devoted years to a project designed to determine whether a computer could be programmed to think like a human. When the team finally felt the project was complete, the anxious experts posed the question they had waited so long to ask, "Can a computer ever learn to think like a human?" The computer responded, "That reminds me of a story." The engineers cried out, "Success!"

Humans have used stories to frame thinking and convey important ideas throughout history. Even today, in this age of technology, stories remain a powerful tool for communication, and a large body of research affirms that people more quickly and accurately remember information first presented in the form of a story (Kouzes & Posner, 1999). As organizational theorist Richard Axelrod (2002) notes, "Universities come to know about things through studies, organizations come to know about things through reports, and people come to know about things through stories" (p. 112).

When Kerry Patterson and his colleagues (2008) examined the factors that had the greatest impact on influencing human thinking and behavior they found that "people change how they view the world through the telling of vibrant and credible stories" (p. 57). They conclude that "a well-told narrative produces concrete and vivid detail . . . a plausible, touching, and memorable flow of cause and effect that can alter people's view of the various actions or beliefs" (p. 61); Nicholas Jay Myers has created such a narrative.

Getting District Results: A Case Study in Implementing PLCs at Work™ is filled with the concrete examples and vivid details that are vital to helping educators alter their view of their schools, their students, and themselves. Myers presents the compelling story of one of America's most successful districtwide initiatives since 2000 to raise student achievement. He explains how educators in Schaumburg Township School District 54 in suburban Illinois have transformed their very traditional schools into high-performing professional learning communities (PLCs), and he examines the impact of that transformation on both the district's students and the educators who serve them. It is a story that has much to offer any educator interested in helping students learn at higher levels.

The Steak *and* the Sizzle

What makes us most excited about *Getting District Results* is that it goes far beyond presenting an inspirational story of one district. Veteran educators who have dutifully gathered together each year to hear motivational speakers at convocation ceremonies or back-to-school assemblies are accustomed to hearing inspiring stories, but they recognize that these events rarely offer them any insights as to what they might do, immediately, to improve conditions for teaching and learning. Even if the message was entertaining, they leave asking, "So what? What now? How will this help us improve our classrooms and our school?"

The best thing about *Getting District Results* is that Myers fills every chapter with proven strategies that provide answers to those questions. He recognizes that educators who attempt to implement the PLC process will inevitably confront formidable challenges, and he provides specific recommendations and actionable steps to help them meet those challenges.

Every school or district that has become a PLC has had to address the following questions:

- How do we introduce the PLC process to educators throughout the district and build support for moving forward with implementation?

- How can we reach consensus about the fundamental purpose of our school, the kind of school we hope to become, the commitments that we must honor to create such a school, and the long- and short-term goals that will both motivate and challenge us?

- How can we foster a collaborative culture throughout our district and throughout our school?

- What structures must we create to support collaboration?

- How can we provide educators with time to collaborate?

- How should we respond to conflict within and among teams?

- How can we determine the most essential things our students must learn?

- How can we use assessment to better meet the needs of individual students and to inform and improve professional practice?

- What are reasonable expectations for students with special needs?

- How can we be more timely, directive, precise, and systematic in providing students with additional time and support when they struggle and enrichment when they are already proficient?

- What changes must occur in our master schedule to support the PLC process?

- How can we ensure alignment between curriculum, instruction, and assessment in every classroom?

- What are the elements of the PLC process that must be tight, that is, nondiscretionary?

- How do we sustain the effort needed to keep the PLC process going?

- How can we learn from other schools both within our district and outside of it?

- What are traditional practices we should reconsider, modify, or abandon because they do not align with the PLC process?

- How do we provide the right levels of accountability and support for people throughout our organization?

Myers addresses each of these questions and many more. It is as if he is saying to his readers, "Be aware that you are likely to face this challenge as you implement the PLC process, and when you do, here is a specific strategy that will help you address it." He also integrates the voices of teachers and principals throughout the book. Their accounts, insights, and advice, presented with conviction and candor, will resonate with educators facing similar issues.

One of our favorite parts of the book is the Lessons Learned section that appears in every chapter. Myers presents those lessons with the wisdom that can only come with experience, but it is his attention to translating that experience into a conceptual framework that offers guidance to other educators that transforms it from an interesting account of one district's success to a vital resource for every school and district.

A Framework, Not a Recipe

The PLC process cannot be reduced to a simple recipe. There is no formula that promises if you add a dash of collaboration and a pinch of intervention you too will improve student learning in your school. The process is nonlinear and heuristic. It demands constant attention to the unique context of the school and district. It requires an action orientation and a willingness to learn through trial and error.

And yet those who are in the early stages of the journey can benefit from the experiences of others who are further along the path. Educators increase their likelihood of forward movement when they have been alerted to benchmarks and signposts to help mark their progress. Myers offers the insights and provides the benchmarks from the perspective of a reflective educator who has been fully engaged in the implementation of the PLC process from the moment of its inception in his district. He has led the process at the building level as a principal and at the district level as an assistant superintendent. He gets it. His respect and affection for educators, his awareness of the challenges they face, and the expertise he has acquired in successfully confronting those challenges makes *Getting District Results* a terrific resource. We recommend it as one of the best books ever written on how to implement the PLC process throughout an entire school district. It should be required reading for superintendents and principals.

introduction

All children can learn. When educators truly embrace this core belief and openly demonstrate it to students, parents, and to each other, dramatic improvements in academic performance result. While it is certainly true that all children are capable of academic success, it is also true that learning happens at different rates. The accountability movement ushered in by No Child Left Behind has required educators to closely examine the instructional models they use to support students from all demographic backgrounds. If we subscribe to the foundational belief that all children can learn, it is our collective responsibility to devise innovative approaches that adjust time and support to ensure that all students do learn.

This book tells the story of one district—Schaumburg Township School District 54—that used an innovative approach to successfully transform itself into a place where all students can and do learn. The district transformed itself into a *professional learning community* (PLC)—"an ongoing process in which educators work collaboratively in recurring cycles of collective inquiry and action research to achieve better results for the students they serve" (DuFour, DuFour, Eaker, & Many, 2010, p. 4). PLCs operate under the assumption that the key to improved student learning is the continuous, job-embedded learning of educators (DuFour, DuFour, Eaker, & Many, 2010). The PLC at Work™ model is based on three big ideas (DuFour, DuFour, & Eaker, 2008):

1. **Big idea one**—The fundamental purpose of the school is to ensure that all students learn at high levels. In order to make this a reality, educators work collaboratively to answer four critical questions: What is it we want our students to know? How will we know if our students are learning? How will we respond when students do not learn? And how will we enrich and extend the learning for students who are proficient?

2. **Big idea two**—If educators are to help all students learn at high levels, they must work together collaboratively to meet student needs. This means that educators are organized into meaningful teams, they have regular time for collaboration built into their schedules, they are clear about the reasons they are collaborating—their purposes and priorities—and that administration supports the efforts of these teams.

3. **Big idea three**—Educators must be results oriented. They must strive for evidence of student learning that they will then use to steer continuous improvement efforts.

District 54 leaders believed that undertaking the process of becoming a PLC would lead to the significant and sustained school improvement necessary to increase achievement for all students across the district.

Schaumburg Township School District 54

School District 54 is the largest elementary school district in the state of Illinois. With twenty-one elementary schools, five junior highs, and a K–8 school of choice, the district serves over fourteen thousand students of diverse demographic backgrounds. In the fall of 2005, the district decided to begin the PLC transformation.

Prior to the PLC transformation, 76 percent of students in District 54 met or exceeded state standards in reading and 80 percent of students met or exceeded state standards in math. However, analysis of district subgroup performance in 2005 confirmed that these statistics hid the following realities:

- Only 45 percent of Individualized Education Program (IEP) students met state academic standards in reading, and only 60 percent met state academic standards in math.

- Only 68 percent of Limited English Proficiency (LEP) students met state academic standards in reading, and only 58 percent met state academic standards in math.

- Only 53 percent of free- and reduced-lunch students met state academic standards in reading, and only 50 percent met state academic standards in math.

- Only 67 percent of Hispanic students met state academic standards in reading, and only 61 percent met state academic standards in math.

- Only 55 percent of African American students met state academic standards in reading, and only 55 percent met state academic standards in math.

Additionally, analysis of state assessment data from 2005 indicated that twelve District 54 schools performed below the state average in reading and/or math.

Within six years of initial implementation of the PLC process, student academic performance improved dramatically with 90.8 percent of students meeting or exceeding state standards in reading and 94.6 percent of students meeting or exceeding state standards in math in 2011. This represents an increase of over 2,100 more students meeting state standards districtwide, compared to 2005, the school year when PLC implementation began. Over that same time span, District 54 moved from the rank of 241 among elementary school districts in the state of Illinois to 65th. Individual school results further demonstrate PLC success. Before 2006, no school in District 54 held the distinction of having 90 percent of its students meeting or exceeding state standards in reading and math as measured by the Illinois Standards Achievement Test (ISAT). During the first year of PLC implementation, four schools attained 90/90 status. Within three years, ten schools achieved 90/90 status, eleven by four years, sixteen by five years, and seventeen by six years.

In 2011, the Illinois State Board of Education recognized thirteen District 54 schools as winners of the Academic Excellence Award for demonstrating sustained results in academic achievement. Prior to 2008, no school in the district had ever been recognized with this honor. Table I.1 and figure I.1 (page 4) show District 54's dramatic achievement gains since 2005.

Table I.1: ISAT Data—Percentage of Students Meeting or Exceeding State Standards

	Reading		Math	
Year	State	D54	State	D54
2005	67	76.2	79	80.4
2006	71	82.7	86	89.9
2007	73	85	87	91.9
2008	72	87.4	85	93.5
2009	72	87.5	85	93.1
2010	74	89.6	86	94.3
2011	79	90.8	86	94.6

District 54 successfully transformed into a PLC with significant, sustained results. Ample evidence validates that the district has effectively internalized the core practices and principles at work within the PLC model. The result has been remarkable improvement in students' educational experiences.

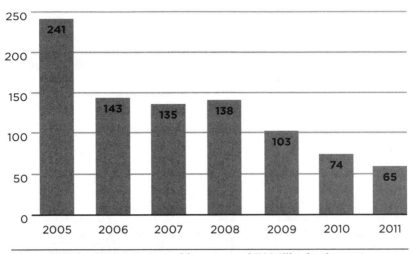

Figure I.1: District 54 state rankings (out of 740 Illinois elementary school districts).

Chapter Overviews

District 54's journey is certainly far from complete, but staff members have learned many lessons along the way. For districts and schools seeking to successfully transform into PLCs at their respective sites, this account of District 54's journey will provide guidance, reassurance, and practical suggestions for ways to develop and enhance PLCs that, ultimately, improve student learning outcomes.

This book provides an understanding of the steps and processes District 54 took and developed to bring about deep implementation of the PLC at Work™ model.

- Chapter 1 discusses the initial steps the district took to introduce the PLC concept systemwide.

- Chapter 2 details the process District 54 used to create its mission, vision, collective commitments, and goals—critical foundational aspects of districts functioning as true PLCs.

- Chapter 3 provides an in-depth discussion of ways to enhance collaborative processes across a school district— from the district office down to grade-level teaching teams.

- Chapter 4 explains how District 54 established essential learning outcomes in all subjects and grade levels through the implementation of a consistent writing process.

- Chapter 5 discusses the importance of writing and utilizing common formative assessments to gauge student mastery of targeted essential learning outcomes.

- Chapter 6 provides an overview of key considerations when building effective systems of intervention and enrichment.

- Chapter 7 outlines key considerations for sustaining the PLC process systemwide over time.

- Chapter 8 highlights the challenges, successes, and lessons learned from principals who have successfully transformed their schools into high-performing PLCs.

- Chapter 9 gives a summary of important considerations for those embarking on the PLC journey.

Key lessons from District 54 appear in the Lessons Learned section that follows each chapter's narrative account.

chapter 1

Building Shared Knowledge

> *Becoming a professional learning community has helped improve the quality of teaching and learning in our school and helped us support the notion that* all children can learn. *We have created a culture of "ours" instead of "mine" when it comes to students. Teachers are committed to working collaboratively to help students succeed. We have created systems of consistency and accountability. We are collectively making better decisions for students because we are working together.*

—ERIN TOSCH, DISTRICT 54 TEACHER

District 54's road to improvement began during the fall of 2005. Superintendent Ed Rafferty believed passionately that the PLC at Work model—developed and advocated by Richard DuFour, Robert Eaker, and Rebecca DuFour—held the promise of bringing about significant and sustained school improvement across the district. Ed shares the four key variables that contributed to his confidence in the PLC framework:

1. The board of education and community held strong expectations for increasing student achievement. District 54 had long prided itself on being a leader in education—yet with the growing accountability movement ushered in by No Child Left Behind, parents and community members were able to now compare the results of each of our schools against one another, with our neighboring districts, and with the state as a whole. The data picture, now transparent to all, demonstrated that District 54 was not producing consistent student learning results across each of our sites.

2. A significant research base supports the PLC as a guiding framework for successful schools. Researchers including Robert Marzano, Richard Stiggins, Mike Schmoker, Doug Reeves, Richard Elmore, Michael Fullan and Andy Hargreaves have all actively endorsed PLC concepts.

3. Professional organizations across the United States endorse PLC concepts. A wide range of professional organizations including the American Federation of Teachers, the National Education Association, the National Staff Development Council, the National Association of Elementary School Principals and the National Association of Secondary School Principals have all endorsed PLC concepts.

4. The PLC model aligns directly with District 54's long-standing commitment to collaborative practices. (personal communication, June 2011)

Providing Initial Training

The first step in District 54's PLC transformation was to build shared knowledge of the process. To do this, the district brought together teacher and support staff leadership teams from all twenty-seven school sites, members of the District 54 board of education, all building- and district-level administrators, and the presidents of both the teacher and support staff unions to engage in a two-day staff development session. This initial training session was critical in building a common understanding of PLC concepts and principles for all stakeholder groups. Specifically, participants discussed the following tenets necessary for schools to function as PLCs:

AllThingsPLC

Visit AllThingsPLC at **www.allthingsplc.com** to read more about the research base for PLC, professional organization endorsements of the concept, and case studies from schools across the United States, as well as to download free PLC resources.

- Embrace student learning as the primary focus and preoccupation.

- Commit fully to creating a *collaborative culture*—a culture in which "people work together, *interdependently*, to analyze and *impact* professional practice in order to improve individual and collective results" (DuFour, DuFour, Eaker, & Many, 2010, p. 1).

- Emphasize *collective inquiry* into best practice—"the process of building shared knowledge by clarifying the questions that a group will explore together" (DuFour, DuFour, Eaker, & Many, 2010, p. 1).

- Value *action orientation* or "learning by doing"—"moving quickly to turn aspirations into actions and visions into realities" through engagement and reflective experience (DuFour, DuFour, Eaker, & Many, 2010, p. 1).

- Adopt an unwavering commitment to *continuous improvement*—"the ongoing cycle of planning, doing, checking, and acting designed to improve results" (DuFour, DuFour, Eaker, & Many, 2010, p. 2).

- Evaluate success and failure by results—not good intentions.

District 54's stakeholder groups developed a shared understanding regarding the importance of the following terms and concepts during this initial training experience:

- Developing and articulating *shared mission, vision, collective commitments, and goals,* which anchor and drive all work in the school district community

- Establishing *high-performing collaborative teams* at school sites that take responsibility for ensuring that students master grade-level appropriate skills and demonstrate this learning in authentic ways

- Analyzing state and district content standards to clarify *essential learning* outcomes—"the critical skills, knowledge, and dispositions each student must acquire as a result of each course, grade level, and unit of instruction" (DuFour, DuFour, Eaker, & Many, 2010, p. 3)—and ensuring that all teachers understand the specific skills and competencies students must master before being promoted to the next level

- Developing *common formative assessments*—assessments created collaboratively by a team of teachers responsible for the same grade level or course—to be administered to all students to determine student mastery of essential learning outcomes and inform instructional practice

Mission, Vision, Collective Commitments, and Goals

Mission: The fundamental purpose of an organization that answers the question, Why do we exist?

Vision: A realistic, credible, attractive future for an organization. Vision answers the question, What do we hope to become at some point in the future?

Collective commitments (or values): The promises made among and between all stakeholders that answer the question, What must we do to become the organization we have agreed we hope to become?

Goals: Measurable milestones that can be used to assess progress in advancing toward a vision. Goals establish targets and timelines to answer the question, What results do we seek, and how will we know we are making progress?

Source: DuFour, DuFour, Eaker, and Many (2010, p. 1–7).

- Developing *systems of intervention and enrichment* to provide systematic supports for struggling students as well as opportunities for extension for students demonstrating mastery of grade-level content and skills

Importantly, the entire district administrative team attended both professional development days and actively participated in all aspects of the training. A portion of each day was devoted to an "ask the superintendent" activity where participants were encouraged to share their reflections and concerns, in order to gain clarity on important questions surrounding the PLC process.

Addressing Concerns and Supporting Teachers

During this activity, many teachers and administrators expressed positive support for the PLC model; however, others expressed their concerns. The most common concern voiced by teachers involved time—specifically, how would teachers find time in their teaching day for the processes involved in PLC transformation? One teacher noted that her instructional day was filled to the brim already, and she wondered if the PLC model would simply weigh hardworking teachers down even further. Another teacher thought that teacher planning time belonged to individual teachers and that if planning time were allocated to "PLC work," teachers would lose time for making parent phone calls, grading papers, and completing other required tasks.

During the activity, other teachers responded to these concerns by vocalizing their belief that, if enacted the right way, the PLC model would help teachers become more efficient in all aspects of their work. Many teachers in attendance had already experienced working on well-functioning collaborative teams, and the PLC model seemed to provide an overarching framework to further guide the processes that these teams were already engaged in.

An additional concern was that PLC would just become the latest fad or initiative for District 54. One teacher noted that she had worked in the district for a number of years and seen many school improvement models and programs come and go. If the district were to be successful in its PLC transformation, the central office would need to limit additional outside initiatives so teachers could really focus on the challenge. DuFour, DuFour, and Eaker (2008) confirm that it is vitally important for a district to limit any competing initiatives during the introduction and roll out portion of the PLC process. Superintendent Ed Rafferty shared with all participants that he would do whatever was necessary to ensure the district's schools would be free to focus on deep implementation of the PLC process.

By the conclusion of the second day of training, participants expressed widespread support and enthusiasm for the PLC concept. Conversations among school teams were already beginning to focus on ways to begin the process at individual school sites, and it was becoming clear that a critical mass of support for PLC implementation was emerging from this guiding coalition of participants.

A pivotal moment occurred just prior to the conclusion of the training when a participant asked Superintendent Rafferty, "Are you saying we will be required to do this? Is this a mandate?"

His answer was vitally important in charting the future course of the district. He responded:

> Why wouldn't we do this? Is anyone aware of any evidence that this is detrimental to student learning, teacher effectiveness, or positive school cultures? This concept is supported by research, endorsed by our professional organizations, implemented with great success in schools around us, and it just makes sense. Knowing the commitment of the teachers in this district to do what is best for kids, how could we not go forward with this? I admit I am not certain as to all the details of implementation, and I will need your ideas as to how we can help all your colleagues become familiar with the concept. I know all of us will need time and resources to move forward, and we will need to consider what we will remove from our plates if we take on this challenge. But this is the work we should be doing, and we need to build on the energy and enthusiasm in this room today and commit to doing whatever it takes to make this happen in our district. (personal communication, September 2005)

Participants then indicated their support for moving forward with this work at their specific school sites using a "Fist to Five" vote—a fist indicating complete opposition to implementation of a PLC, five fingers indicating complete support for moving forward, and numbers in between indicating where teachers fell within this range (DuFour et al., 2008).

No one in attendance signaled below a three, and the vast majority of participants signaled fours and fives. Participants were given the opportunity to express any final areas of concern they had about moving forward. The association president noted that she was in support of this work but believed it would be essential for the union executive board to work collaboratively with district and building administration to resolve implementation issues that were bound to arise. Superintendent Rafferty agreed fully.

Immediately following this initial training, leadership teams at school sites across the district began to develop strategies to build shared knowledge of the PLC framework with all members of their school communities. This involved providing teachers, support staff, and parents who were unable to attend the initial training, with formal presentations so all groups held a common understanding of core PLC concepts. To further ensure common understanding, book studies were organized across the district focusing on *Whatever It Takes: How Professional Learning Communities Respond When Kids Don't Learn* (DuFour, DuFour, Eaker, & Karhanek, 2004). Through engagement in this text and with open dialogue, each school site embarked on the initial steps in their journey of becoming a PLC.

Lessons Learned

1. Train All Stakeholder Groups

District 54 purposefully designed its initial PLC training experience to include all stakeholder groups, including members of the board of education, teacher and support staff union presidents, all district and building administrators, and representative teacher and support staff leadership teams from all district schools. These participants became the guiding coalition in support of the district's PLC movement and were instrumental in moving schools to action in the weeks following the initial training. The superintendent's presence and active participation during the initial two-day training proved important to the successful introduction of the PLC concept overall. This enabled Superintendent Rafferty to learn alongside training participants, listen intently to concerns, provide clarification, and openly state his belief in the potential that PLCs held to positively impact student learning. He clearly supported the PLC vision for future district decision making, and he strategically built consensus among district stakeholders to move forward with implementation of the process. It is important to note that in PLCs, consensus is achieved when all points of view have been solicited and heard and the will of the group has become evident. Consensus in a PLC does not mean unanimity. Districts looking to begin the transformation into PLCs should take time to train broad constituent groups and build shared knowledge before proceeding with systemwide change. Establishing a guiding coalition of supporters is critical to moving the PLC model forward.

2. Prepare for Skeptics

Schools and districts in the initial stages of PLC training will likely face some common obstacles and challenges. As different school improvement and reform models have come and gone over time, educators have grown weary of new initiatives and often approach any initial training experience as cautious skeptics, hesitant to embrace what they perceive as the latest fad. This skepticism can be compounded when district leadership fails to create a shared understanding of the need for change and to explain why the selected change strategy holds promise for success. Additionally, skeptics will continue to bring up the issue of how time will be allocated. Before initial training begins, districts should examine how teacher planning time is currently scheduled and utilized and then be prepared to make a firm commitment to providing teachers with the significant amount of collaborative planning time needed to engage in the transformation. Furthermore, administrators responsible for implementing PLC practices at their respective school sites should attend initial training sessions and remain highly responsive to questions and concerns expressed by their staff. Open and honest dialogue during important, initial experiences with PLC are key to developing trust and moving implementation efforts forward, with the shared belief that all efforts serve the best interest of students.

3. Limit Competing Initiatives

A final consideration for schools and districts beginning the PLC process is the need to limit competing initiatives during the formative stages of PLC development. Transforming into a PLC is an intense and challenging process that impacts virtually every aspect of a school community. The work that faces a faculty embarking on this journey is substantive and significant. Educators should have the opportunity to focus on each component of PLC implementation without distraction. Limiting competing initiatives validates the priority placed on the PLC transformation and enables teachers to commit to the concept in earnest.

Conclusion

Building shared knowledge of the PLC concept and a common vocabulary was just the first step in District 54's journey. Next, the district focused on the critical step of defining its mission, vision, collective commitments, and goals. These components are the foundation of all schools and districts committed to fully embedding the PLC process into daily practice.

chapter 2

Defining Mission, Vision, Collective Commitments, and Goals

The value of creating a meaningful mission, vision, commitments, and goals cannot be overstated. The collaborative process used to create these documents empowers staff to hold themselves highly accountable because they participated in the creation of the objectives. Leaders should not be satisfied with documents that are vague or cliché; they should be a true reflection of the personality and culture of the organization.

—BRIAN LAWSON, DISTRICT 54 PRINCIPAL

People within a PLC are unified by their shared sense of purpose, vision for the future, commitment to enacting positive change strategies, and intention to attain measurable achievement goals. To focus the efforts of the system around PLC concepts and principles, District 54 convened a Board Goals Team during the second year of implementation. This group would be responsible for establishing District 54's mission, vision, collective commitments, and goals that served as the foundation for the district's work moving forward.

DuFour, DuFour, and Eaker (2008) note that shared mission, vision, collective commitments, and goals form the foundation of the PLC framework. They emphasize that in creating a shared mission, an organization articulates its fundamental purpose; in establishing a shared vision, an organization describes its ideal future state; and in establishing collective commitments, an organization explicitly delineates how stakeholders intend to make their shared vision a reality. Setting specific, measurable goals further enables an organization to determine its levels of effectiveness. By establishing such a foundation, organizations provide clarity to stakeholders regarding their intended direction and future focus. District 54's PLC journey proved the importance of establishing such a foundation.

Members of the District 54 board of education were determined that the work of the Board Goals Team be done in a collaborative and inclusive manner. The thirty-two person team was comprised of eight participants from each of the following categories: parents and community, administration, certified staff, and support staff. Parent and community representatives included two board members, three participants selected by the Schaumburg Township Council of PTAs, and three participants selected by a district community advisory committee that had long been in place in the system. The superintendent selected a combination of district- and building-level administrators to represent the administrative team. The Schaumburg Education Association selected the certified staff representatives for this committee, and the Schaumburg Educational Employees Organization (the district's support staff union) selected the support staff. In addition, one student from each of the district's junior high schools was asked to attend a committee meeting to provide student input in the process of writing collective commitments for students (explained in more detail later in this chapter). Including participation from these diverse stakeholder groups enabled the committee to engage in the very collaborative processes that PLCs require.

An outside consultant assisted the district by facilitating the committee's meetings, which included eight in the first year. Having an external consultant facilitate these sessions was extremely beneficial. Superintendent Rafferty noted that the consultant helped organize the agendas for the committee's meetings and assisted in engaging participants in discussions. This outside perspective was particularly beneficial because if a board member or the superintendent facilitates these sessions, participants might be reluctant to openly express their viewpoints (E. Rafferty, personal communication, January 2012).

As the team worked to formulate the mission, vision, collective commitments, and goals that would guide future decision-making efforts in the district, committee members were responsible for regularly sharing information with the groups they represented. These updates ensured that all elements of the school community were kept apprised of the committee's work and progress. Board member Karen Strykowski shared that the team process differed markedly from past attempts to set district goals: "That experience was the first true example of a collaborative process involving all of the stakeholders in District 54" (personal communication, December 2010).

During their initial meeting, the committee took time to develop norms that included assuming positive intent of all participants, remaining focused on agenda topics at hand, and openly sharing perspectives with one another without fear of reprieve. The administration reported on current student demographics, enrollment projections, academic achievement trends, school and district perception survey data from parents and staff, positive behavior programs, and a long-term financial profile. Furthermore, the consultant shared a synthesis of research highlighting characteristics of effective schools and the benefits of a strong collaborative culture. Each member received a copy of *Sixteen Trends: Their Impact on Our Future* by Gary Marx (2006). In this text, Marx discusses emerging societal trends and their impact on student learning. This information was instrumental in helping participants understand how high-performing schools and school districts function.

Distilling Mission

Prior to the work of the Board Goals Team, District 54 had adopted a very lengthy mission statement filled with education buzzwords. According to Superintendent Rafferty, the document "lacked clarity and did not truly galvanize enthusiasm or focus efforts in the system as a whole" (personal communication, January 2012). The Board Goals Team expressed a desire to move toward a succinct mission that was easily comprehensible to staff, parents, students, and the community. A new slogan, "Ensuring Student Success," emerged early on and captured the essence of the team's belief regarding participants' collective responsibility to devise support systems that ensured no child would slip through the cracks. This slogan articulated a sense of shared responsibility and signaled to all that excuses for low student achievement would not be tolerated.

To develop the district's mission, participants reflected on the following guiding questions:

- What is our shared purpose as an organization?
- What is it we expect our students to learn?
- How will we fulfill our collective responsibility to ensure that this learning takes place for all of our students?

The team broke into subgroups to respond to these questions. Each subgroup shared the focus of its conversations with key points captured on chart paper. After all groups reported, a consistent theme emerged: it was the responsibility of the District 54 school district community to work to ensure the success of *all* student learners.

Participants then considered the following statement based on the team's sentiments:

Mission

It is the mission of Community Consolidated School District 54 to ensure student success while fostering lifelong learning.

Slogan: Ensuring Student Success

The consultant asked participants if this was a mission that the group could support; the will of the group clearly indicated that it was. The district's mission had been established.

Expanding Vision

The Board Goals Team next set out to articulate its vision for what District 54 would look like as an exemplary school system in the future. This process began with participants considering and then describing District 54's ideal future state in five years. The consultant referred the group back to the research on successful schools that he had shared at the committee's opening meeting. This helped frame the group's thinking around practices that have been proven over time to produce results for students.

Team members then wrote one-sentence descriptions of District 54's ideal future state on note cards—one idea per card. Members then shared their responses with the group and sorted them into specific categories of related ideas and concepts. Six categories emerged from this process:

1. Student learning

2. Curriculum

3. Instruction and assessment

4. Professional learning communities

5. Parents and community

6. Climate and fiscal responsibility

The team divided into six smaller groups with each subgroup assigned one of the categories. Each subgroup added supporting bullets to its assigned category to identify key points group members shared and then presented its work to the team as a whole. At the conclusion of this meeting, a subcommittee agreed to record the information to create a working draft of the district's vision. At the next team meeting, the subcommittee shared the vision draft with the team (see fig. 2.1, pages 19–21), and the group considered if it was a document all could support. With a clear feeling that the will of the group had been heard, the team's consensus supported moving on.

Vision

To continue as an exemplary district, School District 54 must have a clear sense of its vision for the future. The district is accountable to this vision through commitments made by the board of education, employees, students, parents, and community, and its objective to transform ideals into reality. We recognize that our collective effectiveness in achieving this vision will have significant impact on the learning of our students, the climate of our schools, the sense of professional fulfillment of our staff, and the support of our community. Therefore, we are responsible for and committed to working together to create a school district that exemplifies these elements.

Student Learning

An exemplary district recognizes the importance of each individual student. Employees within the district will make a unified effort to communicate and demonstrate their concern for each student. The result of this unified focus is that each student feels he or she is a valued member of the school community. As the District 54 community, we will:

- Hold high expectations for student achievement with every student meeting or exceeding grade-level standards in all content areas
- Have all students work toward clearly identified goals, collaboratively set with teachers and parents
- Tailor instruction to meet the needs of each student
- Ensure that students not achieving their goals receive regular, timely interventions and support
- Prepare students to participate in a global environment
- Provide opportunities to develop leadership skills
- Foster ethical and responsible behavior
- Encourage critical and creative thinking
- Develop effective multilingual and technological communication skills
- Require students to treat everyone with courtesy, dignity, and respect

Curriculum, Instruction, and Assessment

An exemplary district provides students with a common core curriculum complemented with cocurricular and extracurricular activities. Such a curriculum stimulates intellectual curiosity, ensures students demonstrate that they have learned how to learn, and prepares them to become productive and responsible citizens. The district will clearly state the expectations it has for all students and regularly monitor

continued→

each student's progress using a variety of methods. As the District 54 community, we will:

- Ensure students meet the grade-level standards identified in the essential outcomes
- Differentiate instruction based on student needs
- Insist educators are knowledgeable about and use best practices of instruction and assessment
- Monitor learning on a regular basis throughout the district with the use of common assessments
- Use a variety of intervention strategies to meet student needs
- Employ data-driven instructional strategies
- Fully integrate technology in the curriculum
- Actively engage students in critical thinking and problem-solving simulations
- Teach students how to learn
- Foster culturally responsible and responsive students

Professional Learning Community

An exemplary district is a professional learning community that includes all employees working together on a variety of collaborative teams for the benefit of students. The District 54 board and administration are committed to recruiting and retaining individuals with exceptional expertise in their respective fields. As a professional learning community, all employees will:

- Plan/support instruction, analyze data, and establish intervention and enrichment opportunities in a collaborative manner
- Commit to continuous improvement with knowledge, purpose, and efficiency
- Seek appropriate resources and support
- Be dedicated to continuous learning and student achievement
- Treat everyone with courtesy, dignity, and respect while maintaining all necessary confidences

Parents and Community

An exemplary district understands the importance of fostering effective partnerships with the larger community (parents, residents, businesses, government, and so on). It works to develop community allegiance, support, and ownership in the district. Parents will partner with the schools to support student learning. The District 54 community will:

- Use various forms of communication to share information
- Encourage, utilize, and support volunteers in a variety of opportunities
- Include the community on committees and in decision-making processes

- Offer parent and community education activities
- Provide opportunities to partner with schools
- Expect parents and community members to treat everyone with courtesy, dignity, and respect

Climate

An exemplary district establishes and supports a safe and inviting climate. In all District 54 facilities, we will:

- Create a welcoming and friendly environment
- Ensure all buildings are safe and secure
- Be collaborative, supportive, and professional
- Celebrate our achievements and accomplishments
- Be committed and accountable to the mission
- Maintain an environment conducive to learning

Fiscal Responsibility

An exemplary district recognizes that to reach its vision, it must operate in a fiscally responsible manner. District 54 will continue to:

- Maintain a balanced budget
- Align resources to support board goals
- Maximize the use of financial resources for student learning
- Seek additional sources of revenue
- Ensure checks and balances in the budget process
- Effectively communicate the budget to the public
- Assert an active voice in school funding issues

Source: School District 54 (n.d.d).

Figure 2.1: District 54's vision statement.

Differentiating Collective Commitments

The Board Goals Team next set out to articulate how different constituent groups would work to move the system toward attainment of the district's desired future state. Different stakeholder groups held different roles and responsibilities in the district's quest to ensure student success. To guarantee that the district's collective commitment statements truly represented the feelings of the district's constituent groups, each representative stakeholder group formed its own subgroup to draft commitment statements. Each subgroup identified the promises it would have to make in order to propel the district toward the ideal future state articulated in the vision statement.

The subgroups devoted time to crafting their language before writing their collective commitments draft on chart paper for the group as a whole to see. Because these commitments were specific to each group, other groups were not permitted to change or alter the language. This process ensured that the commitments truly resonated with and connected to the stakeholder groups' roles in the school district. A subcommittee compiled a draft of all the collective commitments, which would be reviewed at the team's next meeting. The district's collective commitments are presented in figure 2.2.

Collective Commitments for the Board of Education

As the board of education, we will use a collaborative process to support the District 54 vision of Ensuring Student Success by our commitment to:

- Celebrate student, employee, alumni, and community accomplishments
- Foster positive relationships with all employees
- Operate in a fiscally responsible manner
- Utilize data to continuously review and evaluate the effectiveness of district programs
- Remain active in the legislative process
- Maintain intergovernmental relationships and networks
- Encourage open communication while recognizing the need for confidentiality
- Participate in a biennial board self-evaluation and ongoing professional development activities

Collective Commitments for Parents and Community

As parents and community members, we recognize that we have the most significant role in shaping the lives of our children. We can contribute to their success and support the District 54 vision of Ensuring Student Success by our commitment to:

- Work collaboratively with school personnel by
    + Engaging in open and timely communication with the school
    + Attending parent-teacher conferences and school sponsored programs
    + Knowing and supporting student goals
    + Advising the school of information that impacts student learning
    + Advocating for our children by asking questions, expressing concerns, and seeking information

- Become informed and knowledgeable about curricular, cocurricular, and support programs available to students
- Require preparation for school and good attendance
- Create a supportive environment for learning by
    + Providing a quiet time and place for study
    + Modeling the importance of lifelong learning
    + Ensuring all assigned work is completed
    + Maintaining high expectations for student learning
    + Insisting on high-quality work from students
- Help our children become responsible members of the school community by
    + Demonstrating respect, consideration, and cooperation when dealing with others
    + Abiding by the school's rules and regulations
    + Modeling responsible, healthy lifestyle choices
    + Insisting they take responsibility for their learning, decisions, and behavior
- Support each other as parents

Collective Commitments for Administrative Leadership Team

As the Administrative Leadership Team, we believe that all students can learn and will support the District 54 vision of Ensuring Student Success by our commitment to:

- Recruit, hire, and retain highly qualified employees who reflect the diversity of our community and embrace our vision
- Establish opportunities and support for ongoing professional growth of all employees
- Support a collaborative culture focused on continuous improvement
- Establish time during the school day for teacher collaboration
- Model behaviors set forth in our vision
- Acknowledge and address behaviors that are not consistent with our vision
- Foster informed and purposeful involvement of home, school, and community
- Maintain a safe learning environment
- Facilitate the development of curricular and cocurricular programs that
    + Ensure high levels of student engagement
    + Address student needs and interests
    + Integrate technology when appropriate

Figure 2.2: District 54's collective commitments.   *continued→*

+ Incorporate grade-level essential outcomes
+ Enable students to understand and appreciate diversity
+ Foster student responsibility

- Systematically monitor student, school, and districtwide achievement through the use of formative and summative assessments
- Make decisions based on data and best practice
- Schedule time during the school day for intervention and enrichment opportunities for all students

Collective Commitments for Certified Staff

As certified staff, we will support the District 54 vision of Ensuring Student Success by our commitment to:

- Hold high expectations for student achievement
- Foster opportunities for students to develop the academic and life skills necessary to make responsible choices, develop independence, and act in a respectful and collaborative manner
- Use the essential outcomes to guide instruction and assessment
  + Utilizing varied and balanced assessments
  + Monitoring student progress
  + Providing differentiated instruction
- Engage in lifelong learning and ongoing professional development
- Share relevant information and implement strategies in our learning environment
- Provide a supportive, collaborative atmosphere where everyone feels emotionally, physically, and intellectually safe while acting with integrity, respect, and honesty
- Actively involve parents in an educational partnership by communicating student progress and educational strategies

Collective Commitments for Support Staff

As support staff, in our diverse roles, we will support the District 54 vision of Ensuring Student Success by our commitment to:

- Create a work environment that is
  + Courteous and welcoming
  + Professional
  + Positive and supportive
  + Safe and nurturing
- Develop and foster collaborative relationships with our colleagues, students, parents, and community
- Participate in effective and respectful communication while recognizing and honoring the need for confidentiality

- Identify and participate in opportunities for self-improvement through professional development provided by the district and other sources
- Model professionalism through
    + Knowledge and performance of job responsibilities
    + Fiscal and environmental responsibility
    + Willingness to consider all opinions and ideas
    + Respect for cultural diversity
    + Personal appearance

Collective Commitments for Students

As students, we understand the importance of having an excellent school district. To do our part, we will support the District 54 vision of Ensuring Student Success by our commitment to:

- Keep a positive attitude and do our best at all times
- Be prepared and take responsibility for our own study habits and test-taking skills
- Be more involved in school activities and encourage everybody to participate
- Accept diversity and get along with others
- Help make our school presentable
- Set, evaluate, and work toward meeting appropriate goals for ourselves
- Share our ideas for helping others by
    + Stepping up
    + Taking action
    + Leading in the right direction
- Accept responsibility for our own education
- Be responsible for our personal belongings

Source: School District 54 (n.d.d).

Figure 2.2: District 54's collective commitments.

Establishing Goals

With newly crafted mission, vision, and collective commitments in hand, the Board Goals Team moved on to the task of establishing specific goals the district would utilize to monitor progress for each of the district's twenty-seven schools.

Prior to the implementation of the PLC model in District 54, district goals were not written in SMART (specific, measurable, attainable, results oriented, and time driven) goal format. For example, a prior district goal stated that "the district will strive to encourage enthusiasm for reading." While admirable and certainly important, this goal was not measurable and was therefore difficult for the district to adequately determine progress toward. The consultant spent time explaining the value of having measurable academic achievement goals in place. Without measurable goals, he pointed out, the district would never be able to quantify progress or lack thereof.

The group came to quick consensus that the district's data showed a need for improvement in reading and math, as well as the need to address the issue of growing achievement gaps among different demographic subgroups in the system; these issues were clear during the first meeting where district achievement data were presented. Several participants discussed the need to have all students reading at grade level by third grade, a critical benchmark year for ensuring future literacy success (Abdullah-Welsh, Flaherty, & Bosma, 2009; Neuman & Dickinson, 2001).

The team hit a crossroads as participants struggled to come to consensus on setting a specific performance proficiency target for all students in the district. Stating and publicizing that the district expected a specific percentage of students to be proficient in reading or math was a challenging notion for many of the team's participants. This would ratchet up expectations in the system and could have implications for administrative, teacher, and support staff evaluations as well as for board members accountable for ensuring the district achieved its stated goals. Team members discussed the different challenges each of the district's diverse schools faced in closing achievement gaps; not all schools in the district were similar in demographic composition, and holding all to the same standard was a frightening prospect to several members of the team. Board member Karen Strykowski noted:

> When we looked at a measurable goal to fulfill the slogan Ensuring Student Success there were some fears from all groups that there would be some students who might never attain that goal, which was based on ISATs, and that our population included a large number of ELL, special education, and low-income students, so how could we be fair? There was discussion across both sides of the debate, but talking it out, we agreed that we had some solid commitments from all stakeholders and that if we set the bar low, we would be doing a disservice to all of our students as well as their teachers. As a group, we finally realized that pushing the envelope would enable us to meet the challenges of NCLB and inspire us. I think that the lofty (at the time) goal of 90 percent meeting and exceeding began the challenge to work collaboratively across the district to find ways to reach all students, to

embrace PLC and recognize that all kids can learn, no exceptions; we just had to be better at finding ways to make that happen. (personal communication, February 2012)

Board member Barb Hengels concurred with Strykowski:

Some were skeptical that setting such a high target was wise or even practical. I was encouraged that those who would be responsible and accountable to meet the target were the ones confident that, while the target was high, it would be worth the reach. They convinced the team that they were willing to work to meet the goal and that their colleagues would do the same. These new goals gave the entire district a focus with strong belief that this was best for students. (personal communication, February 2012)

The team came to eventual consensus around three goals to drive the district forward in the years to come (see fig. 2.3).

Goals

District 54's vision establishes a clear direction for the future. The goals are not intended to stand alone but rather to support the vision and identify the priorities that enable us to answer the question, How will we know if students are succeeding?

In District 54:

- Students who have attended District 54 schools for at least one year will read at grade level upon entering third grade.
- Each school will close the achievement gap for all students in reading and math as measured by both district and state assessments.
- At least 90 percent of all students will meet or exceed standards in reading and math as measured by both district and state assessments.

Source: School District 54 (n.d.d).

Figure 2.3: District 54's goals statement.

In the weeks immediately following the establishment of these goals, concerns emanated from some corners of the system that these goals were in fact unattainable. Staff at different schools in the district openly criticized the idea that all schools could be held to this same standard given the district's demographic diversity. Superintendent Ed Rafferty recalls:

We were forced to really confront our true beliefs surrounding the potential of *every* child to learn and be successful. Setting a consistent, rigorous student performance expectation meant we truly had to take ownership for student learning and start ramping up our systems of support to ensure the success of *each* child in our care. Prior to these goals being in place, we made excuses for why students couldn't be expected to achieve at high levels—our expectations were too low. These goals were critical in shifting those mind-sets. (personal communication, January 2012)

Analysis of District 54's data supports the importance of setting rigorous goals for student achievement as a key step in moving the district forward. At the time these goals were established, no school in the system had ever attained 90/90 status. In the 2011 school year alone, seventeen schools in the system met the district's 90/90 goal. Additionally, in 2011, six District 54 schools (Fox, Frost, Fairview, Link, Hoover, and Blackwell) achieved the remarkable feat of having over 95 percent of their students meet or exceed state standards in reading and math. Without boldly setting high expectations for student performance, these achievements might never have become reality. Today, administrative performance evaluations remain based on these three goals, and school leadership teams continue to utilize them when writing integrated school improvement plans.

Publicizing Results

The District 54 Board Goals Team charted a new direction for the whole district. Upon completion, the team publicized the district's newly adopted mission, vision, collective commitments, and goals to staff and the community through newsletters so all stakeholder groups would know the district's new direction. School faculties took time to discuss these documents during staff development meetings and worked to understand the process in which the Board Goals Team engaged to develop them. Teachers recognized that the district was moving forward with clear expectations for student performance as well as setting forth a clear vision for the desired future state of the system. Framed posters displayed the newly created mission, vision, collective commitments, and goals in all schools and at the district office to further promote the system's new direction.

The process of establishing shared mission, vision, collective commitments, and goals is a key step in charting new direction for a school system's future. In the case of District 54, multiple segments of the district community provided input to define the purpose, direction, and commitments essential for achieving the district's vision. For the first time, clear direction for student performance was established, and the process involved a broad coalition of stakeholders. Strykowski believed the process this team engaged in was crucial to charting the district's future course:

> The group was truly responsible for formulating the vision with emphasis on where we wanted to be in five years. This allowed stakeholders to formulate their group's vision and commitments to support that vision. Every individual and group's input was heard and validated. Because there were such a variety of individuals involved in the process, there was more ownership of the resulting documents and commitment to following the mission, vision, collective commitments, and final goals. Our focus on the goals, which support the mission and vision, has driven our instruction. (personal communication, December 2010)

By publishing and promoting these documents across the system, the district established the "big picture" and set the stage for educational teams at school sites to set student performance goals based on essential outcomes and measured through the use of common formative assessment measures (discussed in detail in later chapters of this book).

Lessons Learned

1. Utilize a Collaborative Process

To successfully implement the PLC at Work model, schools and districts need to take time and build a solid foundation by articulating their shared mission, vision, collective commitments, and goals for evaluating success. Not only will the collaboration process effect substantial changes to key relationships among district participants, generating shared enthusiasm and motivating cooperation, but the resulting documents will also serve to maintain a consistent course throughout implementation. The resulting mission, vision, collective commitments, and goals represent key components to move organizational change forward in meaningful and substantive ways. In examining the work that took place in District 54, it is evident that the collaborative *process* of creating these assertions and documents was as equally important as the end *product* that was developed.

Prior to beginning the PLC process, schools and districts should seek to put together a representative coalition of stakeholders to engage the important work of defining mission, vision, and collective commitments, and setting measurable goals. It is also important to understand up front that the meeting process itself will be challenging. Bringing together diverse constituency groups with potentially conflicting agendas can create inherent tension as planning processes unfold. Involving an outside consultant with experience in facilitating this process will help ensure that meeting time is used efficiently and productively, and that all remain focused on the stated purpose.

2. Assess the District's Current Data

A key step the District 54 Board Goals Team engaged in when developing the district's mission, vision, collective commitments, and goals involved taking time to honestly assess the district's current data. This required team members to examine disconcerting trends and promoted a sense of urgency. Too often, educational leaders excuse low levels of student achievement by attributing poor performance to demographic variables outside the control of school personnel. In District 54, honest examination of data trends illustrated that the district's support systems needed to be revamped. This examination precipitated systemic changes to the way time and support were provided to students in need. These changes became key variables in improving student achievement levels across the whole district.

3. Set Rigorous Goals

The team's decision to set their student performance goals at 90 percent significantly raised expectations across the district. Volumes of research support the notion that high expectations are critical to producing high levels of achievement in all school settings (Hattie, 2009). Schools and districts seeking to set rigorous achievement goals should prepare to respond to doubters in the system that resist calls for accountability and believe they are producing the best results they possibly can—even when these results are poor at best. Evidence from District 54 suggests that setting high expectations ensures that educators take responsibility for student learning and adjust support systems to accomplish desired levels of student success.

Conclusion

The process of clearly articulating a school district's mission, vision, collective commitments, and goals is key to the successful implementation of the PLC at Work model. With these foundational components in place, District 54 focused its energies on moving away from the norm of isolation that had permeated many of the schools in the system and toward embedding truly collaborative processes into the daily work of teachers responsible for generating achievement gains for all students. This component to the PLC model is explored in depth in the next chapter.

chapter 3

Forming Collaborative Teams

Collaborative teaming allows staff to come together and share their expertise as they plan for instruction, problem solve, and reflect. Effective teaming ensures that all teachers are invested in and accountable for all students. Collaboration also allows for strong instruction and continuity as teachers use common skills, strategies, and academic language throughout students' instructional day. Collaboration promotes success for both staff and students.

—JULIE TARASIUK, DISTRICT 54 TEACHER

DuFour, DuFour, and Eaker (2008) emphasize that schools functioning as PLCs organize teachers into high-performing collaborative teams that assume shared responsibility for ensuring student success. They specifically define a team as "a group of people working *interdependently* to achieve a *common goal* for which members are held *mutually accountable*" (DuFour, DuFour, Eaker, & Many, 2010, p. 6). Additionally, they note that effective teams set and adhere to norms of behavior that clarify how to approach team processes. Embedding collaborative processes into schools' daily routines yields many benefits. District 54 sought to systematize these processes at both the district and school levels.

Embedding District-Level Norms

During the first year of implementation, the District 54 administrative leadership team sought to embed collaborative processes into administrators' interactions throughout the district. The superintendent's cabinet initiated this shift by working with the administrative team to set norms governing administrators' interactions. Specifically, these newly written standards of behavior provided a shared understanding of how best to maximize meeting time and encourage productive dialogue among all team members. Collaboratively, the administrative team agreed to the norms listed in figure 3.1 (page 32).

Administrative Team Norms
- I agree to focus on what is best for students; to set aside vested interests and concentrate on the big picture.
- I agree to listen with respect, empathy, and an open mind.
- I agree to honor the individuality of each member and treat others with dignity.
- I agree to give each member the opportunity to communicate his or her ideas without interruption or side conversations.
- I agree to try to understand and appreciate all sides of an issue and the different roles in the school or district.
- I agree to avoid judgmental comments and to critique ideas tactfully.
- I agree to maintain professionalism and confidentiality.
- I agree to support the decisions of the team and facilitate the implementation of team decisions or assignments.

Responsibilities of Each Team Member
- Adhere to team norms.
- Enforce team norms (care enough to confront).
- Be informed of what took place If I am absent.

Source: School District 54 (n.d.d).

Figure 3.1: Administrative team norms and responsibilities.

These norms were regularly reviewed during administrative meetings and included on copies of all agendas distributed to team members.

Additionally, the district encouraged continuous, authentic exchanges among team members, centered on improving student learning. For example, monthly principal and general administrative team meetings moved away from traditional "announcement" meetings to strategic articulation sessions in which team members discussed successes and struggles with PLC transformation. Administrative meetings moved from the district office to selected school locations where principals and teacher leadership teams shared their PLC successes. Following these presentations, administrators reflected on the successes of their own schools and brainstormed strategies to further enhance systemic transformation.

Expanding Feeder School Collaboration

Additionally, principals from feeder schools to each of the district's junior high schools were organized into "feeder school teams." These feeder school teams met regularly to support each other's implementation of the PLC process. These meetings were held at rotating school sites and enabled principals to gain an in-depth look into the way different schools implemented PLC processes. Participating principals set the agendas for these meetings around specific issues and questions facing each school, including how master schedules were developed, how principals were supporting collaborative teaming efforts at their schools, and how systems of intervention were being designed and implemented. Soon, principals began organizing field trips of teacher teams to other district schools so they could learn how to enhance their support systems for student learning. This type of collaboration was an entirely new behavior within the district.

Significantly, these intentional and strategic practices changed the entire focus of the administrative team. Team members began to value learning *from* each other and replicating success stories across the whole system. This cooperative behavior contrasted starkly from traditional administrative cultures that are all too commonly characterized by cutthroat competition and unwillingness to share effective practices. Without question, each of the twenty-seven schools in District 54 competes highly with the others; however, a shared sense of purpose now permeates the system. Principals and teacher leadership teams share their effective practices to enable student success throughout the whole district.

Redefining School-Based Collaboration

For the PLC concept to take hold in District 54, school leaders needed a new concept of teaming. The idea of teachers working together as a team was not new; however, how teams work in a PLC—"*interdependently* to achieve a *common goal* for which members are held *mutually accountable*"—placed a much different spin on the direction teaming would need to take in schools across the district (DuFour, DuFour, Eaker, & Many, 2010, p. 6).

To begin, principals across the system worked with their faculties to build appropriate teaming structures. At the elementary level, this involved setting up grade-level teams and assigning resource personnel (bilingual resource teachers, special education teachers, literacy professionals) to the grade level teams that served students on their respective caseloads. At the junior high level, teachers teamed with those who taught the same courses or subject areas. Resource teachers were again assigned to the teams that served students on their caseloads.

Simply identifying teams in school settings is only an initial step toward embedding collaborative processes in a building. DuFour, DuFour, and Eaker (2008) note that high-performing collaborative teams engage in specific tasks:

- Set and adhere to team norms.

- Set and work collaboratively toward attainment of SMART goals.

- Meet regularly around the critical questions of learning including:

    + Which skills and concepts must students master each trimester?

    + How can our team deliver high-quality, initial instruction that is aligned to our essential outcomes?

    + How can we ensure we share common pacing guidelines?

    + How do we realign time and support for students in need of intervention?

    + How do we extend learning experiences for students in need of enrichment?

Throughout the district, team members were encouraged to focus their meeting time around these key questions so that PLC practices were actively embedded.

Revamping Master Schedules

A major variable the district addressed during its initial stages of the PLC journey involved finding time for collaborative teams to meet and address key issues. Schools functioning as PLCs must provide time for teachers to meet regularly to identify essential learning outcomes, design common assessments, analyze student performance on common assessments, plan for intervention supports, and share effective teaching strategies. Traditional scheduling practices permeated the district when the PLC model was introduced and allowed for limited common planning time for teacher teams. For example, in elementary schools the master schedules were largely controlled by art, music, physical education, and learning center teachers who preferred scheduling all grade-level classes one after another. This practice meant that grade-level teachers never had the same planning period available for team meetings. At the junior high level, interdisciplinary teaming structures had previously been established. This created a scenario where the only teaming taking place happened on interdisciplinary teams that tended to focus on student behavior issues instead of engaging in the critical questions of learning in the PLC model. Teachers teaching the same content and in the same discipline at the junior high level were rarely provided the opportunity to engage in collaborative conversations.

To address this issue, the district developed guidelines for schools to utilize when designing master schedules. These guidelines were "tight" because they provided well-defined parameters and priorities that had to be honored. Specifically, these guidelines required that schools design master schedules so that teacher teams had:

- Maximum opportunities for common planning time
- Designated intervention and enrichment periods
- Uninterrupted blocks for core instruction in literacy, math, science, and social studies

As a result of these guidelines, many schools changed their scheduling models so that an entire grade-level team's students would be engaged in a specials class, such as physical education, music, or art, that provided shared time for teacher teams to meet. Considerable time was spent working with specials teachers to explain why this change in scheduling would benefit students. Specials teachers had grown accustomed to controlling the master scheduling process in District 54's schools and the move toward becoming a PLC altered that dynamic. To address emerging tensions related to this issue, building principals engaged in conversations with their specials teachers to explain why the district was moving in this direction. Additionally, the district established a regular meeting schedule for specials teachers to meet with their own departments.

Furthermore, the district provided additional planning time to teachers by capitalizing on a scheduling practice already in place. On Wednesdays, students across the district were already dismissed thirty minutes early and staff was provided an hour and a half to engage in professional development. Unfortunately, many Wednesday staff development activities lacked focus and were not consistently devoted to examining ways to improve student learning outcomes. Principals across the district began to give this Wednesday time to collaborative teams to provide them with additional opportunities to meet and fully implement the PLC process.

Importantly, District 54 placed a priority on collaboratively determining the final master schedules. Principals in the district were required to meet with their teachers to share master schedule options and brainstorm ways that schedules could be developed to meet the learning needs of students and support PLC implementation. In some schools, scheduling committees were formed to engage in this work; others relied on school leadership teams (elected committees with representatives from teaching staff, support staff, and parents) to engage in this work. This additional example of collaboration was extremely helpful to the district as traditional modes of scheduling were replaced.

Providing Collaborative Team Binders

To ensure effective use of team meeting time, many schools across the district provided staff with PLC binders that helped teams organize their collaborative work. PLC binders typically contain the following components:

- Copies of team norms
- SMART goals for reading and math performance
- Grade-level data summaries from state and local assessments
- Essential outcomes by subject area
- Common assessment calendars for team administration
- Common assessment samples created by the team
- Team agenda templates
- Meeting note summaries of agreed-upon action steps and plans

These PLC binders assisted teams in maintaining strong focus and productive use of common planning time. Today, collaborative teams from schools across the system can refer to their binders to readily produce artifacts and products demonstrating their implementation of the PLC model.

Addressing Fine Arts and Physical Education

One need that District 54 continues to address as it implements PLC processes involves the district's fine arts and physical education teachers. Since these teachers are commonly "singletons" at their school sites, the district had to develop specific structures and processes to encourage their active engagement in the PLC. To do this effectively, the district capitalized on structures already in place.

In the fine arts and physical education departments, a district-level departmental chair already facilitated regular meetings during Wednesday's early release staff development time. As PLC implementation gained momentum in the district, these meetings began to focus on engaging in PLC processes and practices. Initially, the departments set norms and identified essential learning outcomes in their respective fields. With essential outcomes in hand, each department then worked to develop common assessments to be administered at all district schools. Following administration of these common assessments, the departments used meeting time to talk about assessment results, discuss student work samples, and share effective teaching practices and strategies.

To provide further opportunity for the district's fine arts and physical education departments to engage in collaborative processes, the district reserved all districtwide institute and in-service days for the unified arts and physical education departments to meet and discuss the critical questions of student learning. Providing time to apply the PLC framework to their respective fields has helped the district's fine arts and physical education teachers embrace PLC practices. Importantly, the district did not force these teachers into grade-level or content-area teams—these are not natural teaming structures, and forcing collaboration upon teachers who do not share common content would have led to frustration. Instead, the district encouraged fine arts and physical education teachers to engage in the PLC process within their specific disciplines and supported allocating meeting time for these groups accordingly.

Dealing With Team Conflict

Interpersonal conflict among newly formed team members did emerge and does still occur on different teams across the district. One of the great shifts that occurs when introducing the PLC model is the reality that many teachers in traditional school settings have become accustomed to working in isolation. Given that the PLC model requires teachers to engage in deep conversations and collaborative planning sessions centered on improving practice and student learning outcomes, the potential exists for interpersonal conflict.

One district principal shared that during the first year of PLC implementation at his school, one of his teams struggled greatly with the entire idea of collaboration. His three-person "team" had been teaching at the same grade level for several years, but the members had never opened their doors to each other. When informed that they would now be expected to collaborate around the critical questions of the learning, the principal says:

> Each of them approached me separately to let me know they didn't believe teaming together the way PLC requires would work. One teacher on the team was a fifth-year teacher who had felt bullied by the other two veteran teammates for the entire time she'd been at the school. The two veteran teammates told me that they had been forced to teach the same grade level several years back by a previous principal and both were absolutely sick of each other. I met with the team, worked with them to set norms, and even attended several of their meetings. I wish I could say the team saw the PLC light, but I really believe too much baggage had built up between them before we ever even started really teaming. The next year I shuffled them and several other teachers at my school onto new teams, which ended up being beneficial for everyone involved. (personal communication, December 2011)

In virtually every school in the district, building principals had to intervene on at least one team that struggled with moving toward the norm of collaboration. Common themes of discord have included frustration over giving up planning time to work with teachers who are unprepared for team meetings, lack of trust in the teaching strengths and abilities of other teammates, and lack of acceptance of different personality types. Proactively, principals in the district emphasized the need for teams to take the norm setting process seriously—team norms are key to governing the interactions of participants during team meetings. Change is a difficult process and moving from isolation to true collaboration is not easy, but the positive outcomes from successfully doing so are immeasurable.

Embedding Collaborative Practices

Purposefully embedding collaboration around the four critical questions of learning in a PLC has been a key factor in District 54's successful PLC journey. Strategically organizing team members and providing adequate meeting time for collaboration contributed to the successful rollout of the PLC model in District 54. Today, teachers across the system credit collaboration and teaming with dramatically improving students' educational experiences. Teacher Sarah Ortloff comments:

> Working in a collaborative team is absolutely essential to serving families and helping children achieve academic excellence. Each teacher has his or her own unique strengths and talents to bring to the table. By working as a collaborative team, we are able to take those individual strengths and

use them to improve the instruction for the whole grade level or school. Ideas become clarified, instruction is shored up, our craft honed, and we grow as professionals. Sir Isaac Newton said, "If I have seen a little further it is by standing on the shoulders of giants." A PLC is like that: we rise to new heights, raised there by our colleagues, becoming far more as a team than we could ever be alone. (personal communication, August 2009)

District 54 teacher Priscilla Buchanan provides further support for the value of collaboration noting:

Since we have committed to working collaboratively, my grade-level team has a common purpose for instruction and a focus on student progress. We know *what* we are teaching, *how* instruction will be delivered, and *how* students will be assessed. Our common planning time is used effectively by analyzing data and discussing students' progress. During this time, we also plan lesson delivery and put action plans into place for students who are not making progress. The data we collect allows us to speak knowledgeably about our students' progress. All of this is possible because our team has committed to being transparent and believes in the benefits of working collaboratively. (personal communication, August 2009)

Collaborative teaming is central to the work of PLCs. As schools and districts seek to refine their team processes, common concerns and questions inevitably emerge, including:

- How will our teams be organized?
- When will our teams be provided time to meet?
- How will individual planning needs be balanced against the team's need to meet?
- What are our teams expected to produce for administration during collaborative planning meetings?

As teachers become more comfortable working in collaborative teams, these concerns subside. Gradually, teachers realize that time is more efficiently utilized when teams share responsibilities for lesson planning and answering the critical questions of learning.

Lessons Learned

1. Build Appropriate Teaming Structures

For the PLC process to unfold smoothly, schools must establish appropriate teaming structures. Building appropriate structures may involve assigning all grade-level or same-content teachers to respective teams. Schools should avoid forcing teaming structures that do not naturally fit. Building appropriate teaming structures ensures that teams use common planning time efficiently and effectively.

2. Revamp the Master Schedule

Teacher teams must have adequate time to meet and engage in collaborative conversations centered on improving student achievement. Schools and districts that revamp their master schedules can anticipate concerns from specials teachers whose routines will likely be affected. Additionally, schools and districts should be prepared to respond to teachers' concerns that team meetings will consume their individual planning time. In both of these instances, building administrators must take time to explain the purpose and benefits to student learning that result from changing traditional scheduling practices. Furthermore, using a collaborative process to design master schedules and achieving consensus prior to implementation may encourage teacher support. Over time, as PLC processes become refined, new scheduling formats focused on providing common planning time will become accepted practice. During transition, the key is to keep staff focused on the positive impact changes will have on both students and teachers.

3. Prepare for Interpersonal Conflict

As teachers begin to engage in collaborative processes, interpersonal conflict may emerge on different teams. The nature of teaming in a PLC requires teachers to engage in important dialogues about student learning. As a result, differences in teaching style, philosophy, and personality may create tense moments. For teams to maximize their effectiveness, members must address such conflicts. In District 54, creating team norms has been crucial to proactively addressing potential conflicts. Teachers on high-performing collaborative teams monitor their own behaviors and place a priority on adhering to team norms. In instances where collaboration falls apart, the building administrator must be willing to meet with the team to resolve differences and move toward amicable solutions. It should be noted that in nearly every building in District 54, team compositions have been changed as PLC work unfolded. Not uncommonly, principals have moved teachers to different grade levels where personality matches were better suited to encouraging effective collaboration. While this should not be a first step, it may be necessary to accomplish productive teaming structures.

4. Model Collaborative Processes

Schools and districts implementing the PLC process should model collaborative processes and structures at all levels. Working interdependently toward common goals enables all departments to maximize the potential skills and talents of each individual employee. Modeling collaborative processes across all levels of a system validates teaming as an organizational value. Additionally, organizational culture improves as employees embrace collaborative processes and experience an increased sense of involvement and connection with organizational goals. Collaborative processes in a PLC are not limited to teacher teams; rather, they should permeate the entire system and frame planning efforts and interactions at all levels.

Conclusion

Embedding collaborative processes into the daily work of teachers is a critical component of the PLC at Work™ model. District 54 took purposeful steps to establish appropriate teaming structures, revamped scheduling practices to ensure time was available for teams to meet, and provided teams with guidance for what topics should be discussed and accounted for during team meetings.

With teaming structures and practices established, the district moved forward with the critical work of identifying the specific skills and competencies necessary for mastery in all subjects and grade levels across the system. The next chapter will explore the district's process for developing these essential learning outcomes.

chapter 4

Clarifying Essential Learning Outcomes

> *Having key learning standards outlined in our essential outcomes helps focus the teacher's energy on what is* essential *versus what is* just important. *It helps guide instruction as well as informing teachers what key concepts students have already covered and what path students will take in the following year.*
>
> —CAROLYN SMOLINSKI, DISTRICT 54 ASSISTANT PRINCIPAL

Ensuring systemwide clarity about the priority learning standards critical for student mastery was a top priority as District 54 evolved in its understanding of how to effectively reculture its schools to incorporate PLC concepts and principles. District 54 closely adhered to the essential learning outcomes (or essential learning) defined by DuFour, DuFour, Eaker, and Many (2010) as the "critical skills, knowledge, and dispositions each student must acquire as a result of each course, grade level, and unit of instruction" (p. 3). Essential outcomes serve as the foundation for designing initial instruction, developing common assessments, and determining which skills teachers need to emphasize during intervention periods for students who struggle. Well-written essential outcomes provide teachers with a road map of skills students must have as they map out curriculum and instructional plans for the entire school year. Instruction and assessment must be purposefully connected to essential outcomes to significantly impact student learning.

District 54 has engaged in two series of essential outcome writing for the core content areas. During the first year of PLC implementation, representative writing teams from all schools and grade levels came together to develop the district's essential outcomes in literacy, math, science, and social studies. The district's initial efforts at establishing essential outcomes proved to be a great starting point; however, feedback from throughout the system suggested the drafted documents lacked clarity and coherence, and some teachers felt the defined outcomes were too numerous. For example, one elementary grade level listed more than forty essential outcomes for science.

The greatest flaw in District 54's first essential outcomes documents was the consistent practice of including an essential outcome for virtually every state standard noted, which was done out of fear of not including an outcome the state dictated teachers to address. This resulted in cumbersome documents that failed to provide teachers with guidance regarding the skills most critical to ensure student mastery. Additionally, there was no uniform process to develop the district's essential outcomes documents in different disciplinary areas. Content-area directors at the district level created essential outcomes writing teams, but there was great variance in the way meetings were structured and what the final products looked like from subject area to subject area. While the district's first attempt at writing essential outcomes may have resulted in a flawed product, the process remained valuable and lent itself wonderfully to the idea of learning by doing.

The adoption of the Common Core State Standards encouraged the district to engage in a structured process of reexamining its essential outcomes documents. Specifically, the district sought to establish essential outcomes that were clearly written, easily comprehensible, and limited in number so that teachers could focus on those skills and concepts most crucial to student success.

Examining the Review Process

Representative teacher teams from all grade levels and schools formed to initiate a review and revision process. Cathy Lassiter, a consultant for the Leadership and Learning Center, assisted in facilitating this work. Cathy began by having the essential outcomes review teams build shared knowledge around Larry Ainsworth's (2003) concept of *power standards*. These are the "knowledge, skills, and dispositions that have *endurance* and *leverage*, and are essential in preparing students for *readiness* at the next level" (Reeves, 2002, as cited in DuFour, DuFour, Eaker, & Many, 2010, p. 4). According to Ainsworth, standards are *not* created equal; teachers do not have time to cover every standard identified by state boards of education. Teachers must identify priority standards to ensure student mastery of skills essential for school success (this year, next year, and beyond), life (concepts and skills that endure), and high-stakes assessments. Each member of the district's review team read Ainsworth's book, *Power Standards: Identifying the Standards That Matter the Most* (2003), and the district provided teachers with professional development around this book.

Dividing literacy, mathematics, science, and social studies content areas, District 54's essential outcomes review teams analyzed the Common Core State Standards documents, the Illinois Assessment Frameworks, in-house district assessment data, state assessment data, and curriculum pacing guides. Review teams used these resources to develop lists of potential essential outcomes in each subject area by grade level from early childhood through eighth grade.

Following Ainsworth's (2003) process for identifying power standards, teachers at each grade level carefully evaluated proposed essential outcomes by asking:

- Which of the standards have the most weight on the state test?

- Which of the standards provide leverage in other subjects?

- Which of the standards are foundational for the next grade level?

- Which of these standards, based on our data, do we especially need to emphasize?

- Which of the standards provide leverage from kindergarten through eighth-grade graduation?

- Which of the standards are enduring through life?

Grade-level teams engaged in thorough dialogue as they evaluated potential essential outcomes against these set criteria. Evaluating each essential outcome in this manner ensured a thorough and consistent process to identify those items teachers truly felt were most critical to student mastery in each discipline and at each grade level.

After individual grade-level teams drafted essential outcomes statements, vertical articulation across all grades served to identify potential gaps, overlaps, and omissions. This process involved each grade-level team, from early childhood through eighth grade, writing their proposed essential outcomes on large sheets of chart paper and posting these on meeting room walls. All group members then took time to read and examine each grade level's proposed essentials and used sticky notes to indicate areas where there may have been gaps, overlaps, or omissions.

After reviewing these notes and discussing them as a group, each team made revisions to its proposed essential outcomes addressing expressed concerns. Healthy discussion and debate took place throughout this process. When these changes to the drafted essential outcomes were completed, teachers conducted a final walk-through of each grade level's documents to ensure that a coherent early childhood to eighth-grade flow of essential skills had been identified.

Importantly, each writing team placed priority on reaching consensus in support of the essential outcomes drafts. Therefore, team members carefully reviewed the final products and, as teachers, considered if they would feel comfortable and confident implementing these essential outcomes in their own classrooms. In each subject area, teams continued their efforts until they arrived at consensus.

Accomplishing Systemwide Implementation

Following approval from the board of education, District 54's revised essential outcomes were published and distributed to staff and the community. At the school level, building principals informed teachers how the essential outcomes were written and challenged teams to align their instruction with these new priority standards. Grade-level teams across the district now utilize these essential outcomes in writing common assessments, which provide data key to determining which students need intervention or are ready for enrichment experiences. Additionally, for each subject area, teachers receive a three-column poster listing their grade's essential outcomes as well as the outcomes from the previous and following grade. Displaying the essential outcomes in this manner has helped publicize these documents and ensure their coverage in each classroom. See figure 4.1 (pages 47–48) for a sample of this document.

It is important to note that while the process the district-level teams engaged in was thorough, the real impact of essential outcomes documents only occurs when grade-level teams at individual school sites use the revised outcomes to focus instructional planning, develop common assessments, and deliver targeted intervention supports. Robert Marzano (2003) makes the distinction between the *intended* curriculum (the standards intended to be taught) and the *implemented* curriculum (the standards that are actually taught). Therefore, principals need to engage teachers in thoughtful review of priority standards to clarify and address any questions they might have, and to ensure congruence between the *intended* and the *implemented* curriculum.

Second Grade Reading (Reading/Listening/Speaking)	Third Grade Reading (Reading/Listening/Speaking)	Fourth Grade Reading (Reading/Listening/Speaking)
Word Analysis/Vocabulary Students will: • Apply word attack skills to read new and unfamiliar words using a variety of phonemic analysis (such as blends, diagraphs, short and long vowels, and r-controlled vowels)	Word Analysis/Vocabulary Students will: • Determine the meaning of words using context clues, prefixes, suffixes, and base words	Word Analysis/Vocabulary Students will: • Determine the meaning of unknown words using word parts (prefixes, suffixes, root words) and context clues
Reading Strategy/Reading Comprehension Students will: • Use textual information experiences and prior knowledge to make predictions and to infer meaning • Identify main idea and supporting details to construct meaning • Summarize the story or text in a sequential order • Identify author's message (entertain/inform)	Reading Strategy/Reading Comprehension Students will: • Summarize and sequence the events in text • Identify main idea and details • Make/confirm/adapt predictions using textual evidence • Make inferences and draw conclusions of generalizations about text and support them with textual evidence and prior knowledge • Identify author's message (inform, persuade, entertain) • Infer character traits/motivation by what they say, do, or how the author portrays them	Reading Strategy/Reading Comprehension Students will: • Predict and support probable outcomes or actions including identifying cause and effect based on the text • Summarize a story, passage, or text using the order of events • Draw inferences about text and support them with textual evidence and prior knowledge • Determine main idea and distinguish between minor and significant details in a passage
Literary Elements Students will: • Identify literary elements of plot, characters, setting, and problem/solution • Differentiate genres including fiction, nonfiction, and poetry	Literary Elements Students will: • Identify the elements of plot, character, setting, and problem/conflict/resolution	Literary Elements Students will: • Determine what characters are like by their actions and how the author or illustrator portrays them • Identify plot, character, setting, and theme

continued↓

Source: School District 54 (n.d.a).

Figure 4.1: Literacy essential learning outcomes.

Second Grade	Third Grade	Fourth Grade
Writing (Writing/Listening/Speaking)	Writing (Writing/Listening/Speaking)	Writing (Writing/Listening/Speaking)
Focus Students will: • Establish and maintain a clear purposeful focus	Focus Students will: • Compose a focused composition with an introduction	Focus Students will: • Establish and maintain a focus in paragraphs as well as throughout the piece of writing
Organization Students will: • Develop paragraphs using proper form (such as topic sentence, details, summary/conclusions) • Use basic transition words to connect ideas and sentences	Organization Students will: • Develop a structured composition (such as introduction, body, and conclusion) with appropriate paragraphing	Organization Students will: • Organize a composition with a clear beginning, middle, and end appropriate to purpose and audience
Support/Elaboration Students will: • Include specific details such as examples, descriptions, or facts	Support/Elaboration Students will: • Use voice that is appropriate for topic	Support/Elaboration Students will: • Use at least two separate and well-balanced reasons to elaborate ideas through first-level supporting details • Use voice that is appropriate for topic, purpose, and audience
Conventions Students will: • Write simple sentences with correct subject-verb agreement, appropriate capitalization, and end punctuation, and spell most high-frequency words correctly		

Finally, District 54 emphasized that essential outcomes should be viewed as working documents that are reviewed and revised on a regular basis as part of a structured curriculum review cycle. In District 54, content-area teams are formed each spring to engage in this work, which involves reviewing state assessment data, reviewing potential changes in the state assessment, reviewing potential changes to the learning standards documents, and soliciting feedback from teachers across the system. This continual process of review and revision assists in optimizing this list to capture the skills and concepts students must master for success. Figures 4.2 and 4.3 (pages 50–51) show samples of District 54's essential outcomes in literacy and math for grades 2 and 8. (The essential outcomes in literacy and math for other grade levels and the outcomes for all other subjects are posted on District 54's website; visit **go.solution -tree.com/plcbooks** for links to these documents.) Districts should be cautioned against simply adopting these essential outcomes as their own. Doing so would remove the process of learning together and working collaboratively, steps that may prove to be more important in the PLC journey than the final product.

Identifying essential learning outcomes is a key component to successful PLC implementation. Districts and schools engaging in the work of identifying essential outcomes should understand at the onset that this work can be challenging, emotional, and frustrating for teacher writing teams. Digging into state standards, assessment frameworks, and curriculum pacing guides can appear overwhelming at times, and wordsmithing a final document may seem tedious. Furthermore, disagreements emerge as teachers attempt to prioritize learning standards and realize that some long-held favorite lessons or units may have to be discarded. However, this process is critical to ensuring consistency and establishing a shared understanding of exactly what students are expected to know and do at each grade level and in each subject area.

Lessons Learned

1. Utilize Consistent Processes

By utilizing a consistent process for identifying essential outcomes, districts and schools give themselves the best opportunity to create documents that truly clarify where teachers must devote the greatest emphasis to their instruction each day. In the case of District 54's rewrite of their essential outcomes, all disciplinary teams examined the same types of documents, charted potential

Reading (Reading/Listening/Speaking)
Word Analysis/Vocabulary

Students will:

- Apply word attack skills to read new and unfamiliar words using a variety of phonemic analysis (such as blends, diagraphs, short and long vowels and *r*-controlled vowels)

Reading Strategy/Reading Comprehension

Students will:

- Use textual information experiences and prior knowledge to make predictions and to infer meaning
- Identify main idea and supporting details to construct meaning
- Summarize the story or text in a sequential order
- Identify author's message (entertain/inform)

Literary Elements

Students will:

- Identify literary elements of plot, characters, setting, and problem/solution
- Differentiate genres including fiction, nonfiction, and poetry

Writing (Writing/Listening/Speaking)
Focus

Students will:

- Establish and maintain a clear purposeful focus

Organization

Students will:

- Develop paragraphs using proper form (such as topic sentence, details, summary/conclusions)
- Use basic transition words to connect ideas and sentences

Support/Elaboration

Students will:

- Include specific details such as examples, descriptions, or facts

Conventions

Students will:

- Write simple sentences with correct subject-verb agreement, appropriate capitalization, end punctuation, and spell most high-frequency words correctly

Source: School District 54 (n.d.a).

Figure 4.2: Second-grade essential learning outcomes for literacy (reading/writing/language arts).

Expressions and Equations

Students will:

- Fluently compute with real numbers
- Solve linear equations and inequalities
- Use and apply proportional reasoning
- Compute and evaluate expressions
- Solve systems linear equations
- Perform operations with polynomials
- Solve and factor polynomials
- Solve and perform operations with radical expressions and equations
- Solve and perform operations with rational expressions and equations
- Apply exponent properties
- Justify and explain the steps used to solve a problem

Functions

Students will:

- Graph and write linear equations and inequalities

Geometry

Students will:

- Solve real-life and mathematical problems involving angle measure, area, surface area, and volume
- Understand and apply formulas and theorems

Source: School District 54 (n.d.b).

Figure 4.3: Eighth-grade essential learning outcomes for mathematics.

essential outcomes in the same manner, critiqued each potential essential outcome, and were asked to state their support of the final products they created. This ensured that the district's essential outcomes were uniform in scope, coherence, and understanding and that the teachers developing the documents could take full ownership in the product and process.

2. Consult Multiple Resources

Districts and schools engaging in this work should use a variety of different resources to identify essential learning outcomes, including state learning standards, the Common Core State Standards, state assessment frameworks, assessment data, and curriculum pacing guides. By examining these documents, teachers will gain a thorough and balanced understanding of the precise skills and competencies students must master in each subject area and grade level.

3. Strive for Consensus

To create essential outcomes documents that are widely supported and actively implemented requires substantial consensus. Teachers engaged in the process of identifying essential outcomes may disagree on various items; this is a natural part of the collaborative process. It is critical, however, that essential outcome writing teams take time to develop consensus around their final product so they can actively support its use. Teams may wish to use a Fist to Five voting strategy to determine consensus (DuFour et al., 2008).

4. Connect Instruction Purposefully

Effective essential outcomes documents only have value if school-level collaborative teams actively use them to guide daily instruction. To ensure that essential outcomes serve this purpose, building principals should engage teams in conversations to evaluate how they are connecting their instruction to these important documents. Principals may request to see lesson plans or assessments measuring student mastery of a given essential outcome to evaluate essential outcomes integration. Effective teams take time to carefully and thoroughly map out their curriculum to ensure they cover and assess each essential outcome during the school year. Only by carefully applying essential outcomes to daily instruction will teacher teams establish a strong sense of accountability for teaching and student mastery of key priority standards across the system.

Conclusion

A critical component to the PLC at Work model involves establishing systemwide clarity regarding the enduring understandings and competencies students must master in each grade level and course. Well-written essential outcomes provide teachers with the information they need to plan high-impact lessons that prioritize the most important skills students must possess prior to moving on to the next level of schooling. Given their importance, teachers should regularly evaluate student mastery of essential outcomes. The next chapter will explore the important role common formative assessments, linked directly to essential outcomes, play in schools functioning as PLCs.

chapter 5

Utilizing Common Formative Assessment

> *Common assessments drive instructional decision making by informing our practice and helping us identify students in need of intervention and enrichment. Grade-level teams meet regularly to review common assessment data and determine how students are progressing towards mastering a particular learning outcome. Our use of common assessments has also allowed for self-reflection for personal professional development. By administering common assessments and analyzing results, teachers are able to identify areas where they need to improve instruction to best help students.*
>
> —CYNTHIA GORDON, DISTRICT 54 PRINCIPAL

Educators in PLCs are hungry for student data. The use of common formative assessments enables teacher teams to discover students' strengths and weaknesses and adjust instruction accordingly. DuFour, DuFour, Eaker, and Many (2010) define common formative assessment as follows:

> An assessment typically created collaboratively by a team of teachers responsible for the same grade level or course and used frequently throughout the year to identify (1) individual students who need additional time and support for learning, (2) the teaching strategies most effective in helping students acquire the intended knowledge and skills, and (3) curriculum concerns, and (4) improvement goals. (p. 2)

These assessments are administered to all students in a grade level or course to determine mastery of essential learning outcomes and inform instructional practice. Furthermore, they provide the following important considerations for schools to address when developing common formative assessments:

- Common formative assessments should be developed, administered, and scored collaboratively.

- Common formative assessments should be aligned directly to agreed-upon essential outcomes.

- Common formative assessments should provide meaningful feedback to teachers regarding the effectiveness of their instruction and how teams can restructure supports to better meet the learning needs of students.

- Common formative assessments should be accurate predictors for success on high-stakes assessments.

In schools functioning as PLCs, essential outcomes clarify what students are expected to know and be able to do. Common formative assessments enable teacher teams to determine whether or not students have mastered critical skills and competencies, and they provide teams with necessary data to identify next steps. In District 54, educators are encouraged to know every child by name and need. Common assessment data enable teacher teams to do so.

Utilizing MAP Testing

District 54 began using formative assessment data during the first year of PLC implementation when Measures of Academic Progress (MAP) testing was instituted in the system. Developed by the Northwest Evaluation Association, MAP is a computer-based adaptive assessment that measures student growth over time (Northwest Evaluation Association, 2012). District 54 educators continue to use MAP testing three times each school year—once in fall, winter, and spring—to assess student performance in reading and math. Collaborative teams at school sites target any student who falls below the 40th percentile for daily intervention. Additionally, students conference with their teachers to set specific learning goals following each MAP administration. Setting goals based on MAP results provides students and teachers with concrete measures to evaluate future progress.

Using MAP supports teachers across the district in learning how to utilize assessment data to inform instructional practice. Prior to the use of MAP, the district lacked valid and reliable assessment data on student performance; state assessment results were truly the only uniform pieces of data schools had access to, and this information told teachers very little about the specific academic needs of their students. MAP provides skill-by-skill analysis of areas of strength in reading and math—data that were not in teachers' hands prior to its utilization. Furthermore, since MAP is administered three times each year, it helps teachers see the growth their students are making over time. These data prove critical during the interim while teachers become proficient in developing their own solid common formative assessments.

Initiating Teacher-Created Common Assessments

While District 54 continues to use MAP as part of its PLC process, there is no substitute for the common assessments that teachers develop directly from curriculum and essential learning outcomes. These assessments give a true profile of a student's learning. During the initial stages of District 54's journey as a PLC, school teams began small with common assessment development focusing only on one subject. Given the district's need to address the key area of literacy, all elementary schools in the system began by targeting reading and writing. Teams were encouraged to identify eight to ten essential outcomes addressed in the district's literacy curriculum during each trimester and design one common assessment per trimester to assess those essential outcomes. By focusing only on one subject area and keeping expectations for common assessment development and administration manageable, school teams gained confidence in their work before addressing additional subject areas and adding additional common assessments. One example of this process took place at Fox School where all teams focused in on formal writing during the school's first year of PLC implementation. Teams developed three writing prompts to be administered to students as common assessments. Teams also developed common scoring rubrics and sat down together to evaluate student writing samples, share effective teaching strategies, and make plans to provide additional supports for students who struggled. This simple process provided a low-stress way for Fox's teams to embark on the collaborative work of being a PLC.

Developing high-quality common assessments was challenging at first for teachers in District 54. There was certainly a learning curve that teams went through with this component of the PLC model. One third-grade team in the district recalls that the first common assessment they administered was a ten-question quiz that simply asked students to circle prefixes and suffixes of root words. The team used the results of these assessments to regroup students for two weeks of intervention on this small, isolated skill. The team quickly determined they were not assessing a rigorous enough skill for their grade level and refocused their planning efforts on writing common assessments that truly were linked to essential, priority learning standards such as determining the main idea of grade-level appropriate text. An additional challenge many District 54 teachers faced in the early stages of their work with common assessments involved aligning initial instruction, common assessment adminis-tration, and intervention delivery. In some schools, teams developed and administered common assessments out of sequence with the specific skills being presented in the core curriculum. This resulted in students both being assessed on skills that had not been thor-oughly introduced during initial instruction and being identified inappropriately for intervention supports. Additionally, the district grappled with the question of how to handle administering common assessments to English learner and special education students. A debate took place around the fairness of assessing these groups and what, if any, assessment accommodations or modifications should be provided for these groups. Addressing these issues was all part of the natural "learning by doing" process. As school teams dug deeper into this work, several quickly gained confidence in the pro-cess and products they were creating. An examination of schools where this occurred follows.

Michael Collins Elementary School

Michael Collins Elementary School staff placed a strong empha-sis on developing a comprehensive common assessment calendar as a part their PLC transformation. Collins teachers carefully exam-ined the district's essential outcomes and, over time, wrote a series of high-quality common assessments tied to these priority stan-dards. The staff believed strongly in the use of these assessments, as reflected in the following comments of Collins teacher Kim Savino:

> Common assessments have helped our team better under-stand the needs of our students. We work together as a team to produce assessments that will provide us with valuable information about each and every student. Having the same assessment, across the board, alleviates many problems. We are now able to diagnose where the problem lies, leav-ing very little room for guessing. (personal communication, August 2009)

Under the leadership of Principal Laura Rosenblum, the Collins staff worked to formalize a structured process for developing and using common formative assessments as part of their initial steps toward PLC implementation. All school teams used the following eight-step process:

1. Teams selected which essential outcomes to assess by using the district-created essential outcomes documents.

2. Teams used common planning time to create a common assessment with input from all members. This process required teammates to determine when a given essential outcome was going to be presented to students in the curriculum. Teammates also brainstormed for the best assessment format given the skills being assessed.

3. Teams mapped out their essential outcomes for the year by trimester. Within the trimester, teams considered the complexity of the essential outcome being assessed to determine the length of time it would take for students to acquire proficiency. They then set an agreed-upon date to administer the common assessment.

4. Following the administration of a common assessment, teams utilized common planning time to collaboratively score student assessments. If common assessments were multiple choice, teams tabulated their results and shared them openly. Teams often conducted an item analysis of multiple choice questions to determine if there were particular trends in areas where students struggled or excelled. Conducting an item analysis also helped teams determine if there were any issues with confusing wording in a given question, which may have skewed student results. If common assessments were open-ended (such as a writing sample) teachers scored their own student assessments and traded papers to ensure all are administering commonly developed rubrics the same way.

5. Teams entered all common assessment data into a spreadsheet, analyzed the data, and formed intervention and enrichment groupings based on the results. Intervention groups were established to provide additional time and support to students struggling on common assessments—a teacher to student ratio of 1:8 was never exceeded. Students meeting proficiency targets on common assessments were moved into enrichment groups to extend their learning.

6. Teams determined a timeline for how long intervention supports would be provided to students who struggled on the common assessment.

7. Teams devoted instructional time for intervention and enrichment supports as they answered the questions: how do we respond to the students who didn't understand the concept we assessed, and how do we respond to students who have mastered the concept we assessed?

8. For students receiving interventions, teams developed and administered a second common assessment after a preset amount of time to determine if the interventions provided were effective. After this second common assessment was administered, teams took time to reflect on the process and share effective instructional strategies. Importantly, teachers with students scoring lower on common assessments were provided the opportunity to learn from their colleagues and use new strategies for teaching specific skills—a hallmark practice in schools functioning as PLCs.

Teacher Cassie Zingler shares that when this process was first presented to the staff, Principal Rosenblum provided teams with guiding reflective questions and planning templates for each step in Collins' process. (Visit **go.solution-tree.com/plcbooks** to see samples of these documents.) This was extremely beneficial in helping teams remain focused on the PLC process. Zingler shares:

> Since creating and administering common assessments was fairly new to our building, teams needed guidance with how to reflect on student data. To assist us in this process, our principal gave us a series of questions to consider and respond to before and after an assessment was administered. These questions prompted my team to dig deeper into students' data. These questions focused us in considering everything from the validity of the test, to our next instructional steps, to how the skill impacted students' overall academic success. As we became savvier with our reflections, this became a natural part of our PLC routine. (personal communication, February 2012)

Furthermore, Zingler notes that the Collins staff placed an emphasis on meeting with individual students to discuss their results on common assessments. She asserts that these conversations were instrumental in providing students with an understanding of where they were functioning well and where they could still grow:

It became a common practice at Collins School to provide students with not only individual data but overall class data. We devoted time for students to provide us with feedback. We were likely to ask students about what they thought made an impact with their learning and about what additional support they feel they might need to continue to make progress. Asking students to reflect had a dual purpose for my team. It opened our eyes to additional steps we could take to ensure all of our students were successful and students were more invested in their learning because they knew their input was valued. (personal communication, February 2012)

Reviewing Sample Common Assessments

Teams within a PLC must develop common assessments on their own and are discouraged from simply adopting other teams' assessments; however, it may help to review common assessment samples created collaboratively by other teams as you begin your journey as a PLC. Teacher teams at Fairview Elementary School created the assessment samples in figures 5.1 and 5.2 (pages 59–63). These samples provide a working example of what quality common assessments look like in terms of formatting and connection to targeted essential outcomes, which are key considerations for determining the quality of a common assessment.

Name _____

Essential Outcome: Determine main idea and distinguish between minor and significant details in a passage.

Read the passage and answer the questions below.

Michael Jordan

Michael Jordan was born February 17, 1963, in Brooklyn, New York. His family moved to North Carolina when he was just a baby. As a young boy, his favorite sport was baseball, but he soon found that he could play basketball as well. At age 17, he began to show people just how talented he really was. Throughout his career, Michael Jordan won many scoring titles and team championships. Many boys and girls look up to Michael Jordan as their hero. Did you know he had a hero when he was growing up too? He looked up to his older brother, Larry. Michael Jordan, a basketball superstar, is not just a star on the court. He also works hard to raise money for many children's charities. He encourages children to develop their talents in whatever sport or activity they love with practice, practice, practice! (Douglas, 2003, page 144)

continued→

1. This story is mainly about:

    A. Michael Jordan's baseball career.

    B. Michael Jordan's life.

    C. The charity work Michael Jordan has done.

    D. Michael Jordan's hero.

2. Which of these is a minor detail in the passage?

    A. Michael Jordan was born February 17, 1963.

    B. He has an older brother named Larry.

    C. Michael Jordan won many scoring titles and team championships.

    D. He works hard to raise money for children's charities.

3. Which would be another good title for this passage?

    A. Player and Hero

    B. Basketball

    C. My Brother Larry

    D. Playing Baseball

. . . .

Read the passage, and fill in the graphic organizer that follows.

Mary Lou Retton

Mary Lou Retton became the first U.S. woman to win the Olympic gold in gymnastics. She accomplished this at the 1984 Olympics held in Los Angeles, when she was 16 years old. "Small but mighty" would describe this gymnast. She was the youngest of five children, all good athletes. She grew up in Fairmont, West Virginia, and began her gymnastic training at the age of 7. Most woman gymnasts are graceful, but Mary Lou helped open up the field of gymnastics to strong, athletic women. To this day, she is the only U.S. woman to win the All-Around title at the Olympics. (Douglas, 2003, p. 145)

Main Idea	Major Details (Write two)	Minor Detail (Write one)
	1. 2.	1. 2.

Why would "A Gymnastic Champion" be another good title for this passage?

_____

_____

_____

Figure 5.1: Fourth-grade main idea and details common assessment.

Name _____

Essential Outcome: Summarize a story, passage, or text using the order of events.

Read the passage and answer the questions below.

Amelia Earhart

Amelia Earhart became one of the most famous women to fly. She was born on July 24, 1897. Earhart saw her first plane at a state fair when she was ten years old. She didn't think it was anything special. She changed her mind about flying once she took her first ride in 1920.

The next year Earhart took her first flying lesson and soon after bought her first plane. It was a bright yellow plane that she nicknamed "Canary." After years of flying, she received an amazing invitation in 1928. She was asked to become the first woman to fly across the Atlantic Ocean.

Earhart traveled as a passenger on her first trip across the Atlantic. She joined pilot Wilmer "Bill" Stultz and co-pilot Louis F. "Slim" Gordon for the journey. News of their flight and Earhart becoming the first woman to cross the Atlantic by plane made headlines around the world.

Four years later Earhart set out on an amazing journey of her own. She decided to cross the Atlantic again, but this time she would be the pilot and the plane's only crew member. She flew from Harbor Grace, Newfoundland, on May 20 and arrived in Paris, France, the next day. This time the trip was even shorter—it took her 15 hours to make the journey. Her adventure brought her international fame.

She wanted to show that women could be great pilots just like men. In 1937, she was ready for her biggest challenge of all, to fly around the world. She wanted to be the first woman to complete this feat. Sadly, she never made it. The plane and crew were lost at sea in the middle of the journey. She will be remembered forever for her courage and bravery. (Adapted from BIO Classroom, n.d.)

1. According to the passage, which of these events happens first?
   A. Amelia Earhart crossed the Atlantic alone.
   B. Earhart bought her first plane.
   C. Amelia and two male pilots flew across the Atlantic.
   D. Amelia took a flying lesson.

2. Which event happens before she was the first woman to fly across the Atlantic?
   A. Amelia didn't think flying was anything special.
   B. Earhart's plane and crew were lost at sea.
   C. Earhart took a 15-hour journey.
   D. She arrived in Paris, France.

Figure 5.2: Fourth-grade summarize and sequence common assessment.

continued→

3. According to the passage, which event goes in the empty box?

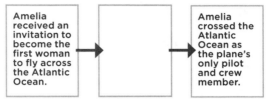

A. Amelia's plane and crew disappeared.

B. Earhart traveled as a passenger across the Atlantic.

C. Amelia was remembered for her courage and bravery.

D. Amelia went on a 15-hour adventure.

4. Which would be the best summary of this passage?

A. Earhart crosses the Atlantic many times in the plane she bought.

B. Amelia Earhart changed the world of women in flight through her courage and bravery.

C. Amelia Earhart died in a plane crash.

D. Amelia Earhart took a flying lesson then bought herself a plane.

· ·

Read the directions, and answer the questions that follow.

Lemonade Stand

Have you ever dreamed of earning money? Here is one great idea! Make your own lemonade stand! Read to find out how to go into business.

Things you'll need:

- Long spoon
- Cooler
- Lemons
- Paper or plastic cups
- Cold water
- Pitcher
- Sign
- Sugar
- Table and chair

Instructions:

1. Set up your lemonade stand at the end of your driveway or on a sidewalk where there are many people walking and driving by.

2. Decide when the busiest times of day or weekend are. This is when you will sell the most lemonade.

3. Set up your stand. Write the price on a large sign. Make sure to have your cups on hand. If you are going to be outside for a while, make sure you have a cooler filled with ice.

4. Buy sugar and lemons and make lemonade. In a large pitcher, combine the lemon juice, sugar, and cold water; stir quickly to dissolve. Add ice cubes.

5. Price your lemonade to cover all your costs and so you have some money left over.

6. Sell your lemonade!

(Adapted from eHow.com, n.d.)

1. Which event must happen after you buy the lemons and sugar?

   A. Set up your stand.

   B. Make a large sign.

   C. Combine the lemon juice, water, and sugar.

   D. Choose a day and time for your stand.

2. According to the passage, what happens first?

   A. Stir the mixture quickly.

   B. Decide on the price of your lemonade.

   C. Choose a day, time, and place to sell your lemonade.

   D. Sell your lemonade.

3. According to the text, which event belongs in the empty box?

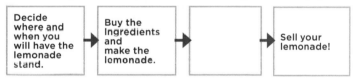

   A. Make a large sign to advertise your lemonade.

   B. Decide on the price of your lemonade.

   C. Buy disposable cups.

   D. Ask your friends to taste-test your lemonade.

4. Write a new title that would summarize this passage.

_____

_____

_____

Figure 5.2: Fourth-grade summarize and sequence common assessment.

Well-designed, team-created common assessments can provide teachers with a wealth of information regarding the specific learning needs of their students. District 54 teams have continued to work at this component of the PLC at Work model and students are reaping the benefits as a result.

Lessons Learned

1. Start Small With Ongoing Support

In PLCs, leaders must provide teachers with ongoing support and assistance to develop common assessments that supply accurate data regarding student proficiency of targeted essential learning outcomes. Starting with one subject area and asking teams to create only one common assessment per trimester during the first year of PLC implementation benefited District 54. Starting small allowed teams time to familiarize themselves with the entire process and prepare for future success. Schools beginning the PLC transformation should examine their assessment data to determine the area of greatest need and then establish consistent, manageable expectations for all grade levels. As teachers become more fluent with developing quality common assessments, teams can tackle the challenge of creating additional assessments.

2. Develop Common Assessment Calendars

Schools implementing common assessments should require collaborative teams to establish common assessment calendars that identify the essential outcomes teachers will cover and assess each month throughout the school year. Teams should also include district and state mandated assessments on these calendars so that administration of in-house common assessments does not interfere with high-stakes testing. Ultimately, teams should develop a comprehensive common assessment plan that ensures each subject area essential outcome is taught and assessed at an appropriate time during the school year. In the PLC at Work model, teams are expected to assess each essential outcome identified; this will occur over time as teams engage in the process. Given the complexity of this component of the PLC model, administrators must provide time, support, and guidance to teacher teams as they engage in this work.

3. Accommodate Students With Special Needs

A recurring theme emerged across District 54 as collaborative teams began developing and administering common assessments. Some teachers resisted administering common assessments to bilingual students or students with individual education plans (IEPs). In some instances, teachers sought to modify common assessments for these students. However, district leaders wanted to ensure high expectations for all learners. Therefore, the district mandated that all students complete the same common assessments at a given grade level. This is the only way to ensure that teams have accurate, valid, and reliable data on each student's learning. Teachers should be

discouraged from modifying common assessments beyond providing accommodations as noted in a student's IEP.

4. Align Instruction, Common Assessment, and Intervention

One challenge that District 54 faced when implementing common
assessments involved teachers developing and administering assessments that were not in sequence with skills covered during initial
instructional periods. This resulted in students being assessed for
skills they had not yet been taught during initial instruction or intervention. To address this problem, the district provided the following
tight (nonnegotiable) expectations:

- Grade-level teams provide consistent initial instruction utilizing the district's adopted curriculum. This is important to
  ensuring all students are exposed to what Robert Marzano
  refers to as a "consistent and viable curriculum" (2003).

- Teams develop common assessments in alignment with
  the district's essential outcomes and the scope and
  sequence of skills addressed in the district's adopted
  curriculum.

- Teams use the results of common assessments to trigger
  the intervention system (discussed in more detail in the
  next chapter).

  + Teachers should focus their instruction during
    interventions on providing an extra dose of time
    and support for the same skills, concepts, and
    vocabulary addressed during initial instruction.
    Teachers should provide a different instructional
    strategy during intervention time to increase the
    likelihood of student learning.

  + Teams need to maintain a careful focus on align-
    ing initial instruction, common assessment, and
    interventions. Failing to coordinate these pieces
    will result in fragmented instruction for the
    neediest students.

Conclusion

Common formative assessments—created by collaborative teams
and tied to essential learning outcomes—provide important data
regarding student mastery of skills critical to school and life success. The only way to truly know the specific learning needs of each

student is to take time to assess their mastery of targeted skills on an ongoing basis. Once teams of teachers have these data in hand, important decisions need to be made about ways to provide additional time and support to students in need as well as to provide enrichment experiences to students mastering grade-level-appropriate skills and content. These systems of intervention and enrichment are explored in the next chapter.

chapter 6

Establishing Systematic Intervention and Enrichment

> *The utilization of intervention systems has allowed us to target student areas of growth and has brought systemic change when we evaluate how we can close achievement gaps. Intervention systems used by our school allow us to target instructional deficits and foster the art of conversation among our staff as we talk about our students. The use of intervention systems has been the single most pervasive way to positively impact student achievement at Hoover Math and Science Academy.*
>
> —JAKE CHUNG, DISTRICT 54 PRINCIPAL

As District 54 steadily refined its instructional systems to incorporate PLC processes, district and school leaders specifically emphasized the need for districtwide consistency regarding interventions for struggling students. DuFour, DuFour, Eaker, and Karhanek (2010) urge schools to develop systems of intervention that are:

- Systematic in identifying students by *name* and *need*
- Built into the structure of the school day
- Guaranteed to *all* students demonstrating difficulty mastering grade-level appropriate material
- Delivered as an "extra dose" on top of initial instruction—not as a replacement for initial instruction

Using these guiding principles as a foundation, schools across the district began to revamp their master schedules to provide common planning time for grade-level teams and to identify uninterrupted blocks of time for initial instruction and targeted intervention periods.

Learning by Doing

Individual District 54 schools initially designed their intervention systems in different ways and with varying degrees of success. Several schools began by simply having all classroom teachers stop initial instruction during the same thirty-minute period each day for intervention time. Students generally remained in their same classroom doing seatwork while their teacher worked with a small group for extra support. This meant struggling students never benefited from working with any teacher other than their homeroom teacher—even when common assessment data may have indicated a different teacher on the team was producing stronger results in terms of student mastery of given skills. This also meant students who were not targeted for intervention were simply completing seatwork instead of having their learning truly enriched.

Several schools relied heavily on the use of scripted intervention programs, which lacked clear connection to content being presented during initial instruction and took a "one size fits all" approach to remediating struggling students. The PLC process calls on teachers to be reflective in their work, share effective teaching strategies, and use shared expertise to impact learning—simply turning to a boxed program to "fix" students in need undermines the PLC process entirely.

During the district's initial foray into intervention work, the only tight expectation in place required all schools to build intervention periods into daily instructional routines. Over time, numerous schools across the district vividly demonstrated how more intricately designed intervention systems could lead to dramatic gains in student academic achievement. These models then became replicated across the system, resulting in demonstrable gains in student achievement across the district as a whole. An examination of such systems follows.

Applying Literacy Intervention

District 54 schools all began their work with interventions by focusing on reading and writing, as state assessment data demonstrated that these were the major priority areas for the district. For years, the district had relied on the use of instructional assistants to pull struggling readers out of literacy blocks, utilizing scripted remediation programs to attempt to close achievement gaps. These approaches were unsuccessful as students were consistently pulled out of initial core literacy instruction (thus denying them exposure to rigorous, grade-level appropriate curriculum), instructed by noncertified teaching staff, and treated as if each student had the same learning difficulties impacting them in the classroom. This approach falls in stark contrast to the systematic and timely approach to intervention advocated in the PLC at Work model. Two District 54 schools, Anne Fox and Fairview, were frontrunners in designing literacy intervention systems that accounted for the key principles advocated in the PLC process. An explanation of these models follows.

Anne Fox Elementary School

Anne Fox Elementary School is a moderately low-income, demographically diverse, targeted assistance Title I school located in the working-class suburb of Hanover Park. The Anne Fox student population is 34 percent white, 35 percent Hispanic, 18 percent Asian, and 9 percent African American, 4 percent multiracial, and less than 1 percent Native Hawaiian/Pacific Islander and American Indian (School District 54, n.d.c). More than thirty-five different languages are represented at Fox, and the building's low-income and mobility rates are more than double the district average. Until the first year of implementation of PLC processes, Anne Fox ranked last in academic achievement among the twenty-one elementary schools in District 54. However, incorporating new systems of student support changed this trend, and the building has experienced unprecedented gains in overall student achievement as measured by the ISAT. For example, in reading, Fox moved from 59 percent of students meeting or exceeding state standards the first year of PLC implementation to 98.4 percent of students meeting or exceeding state standards six years later. In math, the school moved from 76 percent of students meeting or exceeding state standards the first year to 97.9 percent six years later. Furthermore, achievement gaps among demographic subgroups virtually disappeared.

Prior to the start of their PLC journey, Fox faculty experienced great frustration over repeated low student performance on local and state assessments. Over time, the school's reputation had become marred, and the building came to be known as a "problem spot" within the district. The school lacked effective systems to intervene with students exhibiting difficulty mastering grade-level appropriate concepts and skills. Several ineffective practices contributed to this breakdown. Specifically, faculty did not have well-designed formative assessments to collect authentic data regarding grade-level essential outcomes. Individual teachers largely fended for themselves in determining how to assess student progress or grade-level proficiency in targeted areas. Without reliable data, teams struggled to develop intervention strategies. In short, grade-level teams at Fox did not consistently focus on results.

Additionally, staff at Fox relied solely on outdated and ineffective modes for supporting students struggling to grasp essential skills. Prior to their PLC transformation, the school had three main responses for remediation: (1) afterschool tutoring groups, (2) group pull-out instruction using a canned literacy remediation program administered by an instructional assistant, and (3) referral to the school's special education Child Study Team. For years, students languished with these ineffective responses, and the building inched dangerously close to failing to meet adequate yearly progress as dictated by No Child Left Behind.

To change this disturbing trend, the staff began by first considering if they clearly identified the essential outcomes in core academic areas that all children must have in place before moving along to the next grade level (as discussed earlier in chapter 4). Next, they developed meaningful formative assessments that truly identified the specific learning needs of each child (as discussed in chapter 5). After that, they examined the following three questions:

1. Do we intervene the moment *any* child demonstrates difficulty mastering essential grade-level skills and concepts, or do we wait until children fail before placing them into intervention programs?

2. Are our interventions by invitation, or are they systematically built into our 8:40 a.m. to 3:00 p.m. school day and delivered to *all* students in need of additional time and support?

3. Do we wait until a child has an IEP before we provide additional time and support?

To accomplish change, Fox needed to devise new systems of both instruction and support for all students, especially those students struggling to master essential outcomes. The first critical discussion that took place on the Fox campus involved teachers committing themselves to creating serious academic learning environments, including a daily, ninety-minute minimum literacy block for all children. During this ninety-minute block, teachers implemented a comprehensive, balanced literacy model (developed by the District 54 Department of Instruction) calling for daily guided, shared, and independent reading and writing, as well as vocabulary and word study instruction. Implementing a new literacy model ensured that all children received high-quality initial instruction from grade-level teachers.

The district established an additional expectation for the ninety-minute literacy block: initial literacy instruction took precedence over all other student activities. All educators adopted the attitude that no student could afford to miss this instruction. This expectation required that teachers abandon the outdated and ineffective practice of pulling students out for remedial instruction during initial instruction. Instead, students received support in the classroom from resource teachers who shared responsibilities with regular education classroom teachers by pushing supports in and co-teaching lessons. This practice ensured that all children received grade-level curriculum with an appropriate level of academic rigor.

Once all students were receiving high-quality initial literacy instruction in whole-class settings, grade-level teams administered regular common formative assessments to determine students' specific learning needs. With regular monitoring of student mastery of essential skills, grade-level teams could effectively identify which students needed intervention and which students were ready for enrichment.

To provide an intervention and enrichment block of time during the school day, administrators established a forty-five-minute period on the master schedule for each grade-level team. They called this a "parallel block." During parallel block, all new instruction stopped and students regrouped by instructional need across the grade-level team. Students needing additional time and support to master a skill or concept moved to a classroom where they received structured, small-group intervention with an adult-to-student ratio that never exceeded 1:8. By mobilizing special education resource staff, bilingual resource staff, the building's literacy coach, and an instructional assistant, student support teams flooded services into the team at a regular time each school day. Similarly, students having mastered skills on common assessments regrouped for enrichment instruction in a whole-class setting.

Teachers used a wide variety of instructional practices during Fox's daily parallel block, including additional guided reading time, vocabulary lessons, and mini-lessons in formal writing to enhance skill mastery for students identified as needing intervention. Likewise, students working in enrichment blocks benefited from differentiated instruction at their appropriate learning levels, including literature circles involving on-level texts and independent research projects. Importantly, the staff quickly recognized the need for students in both intervention and enrichment groups to be provided with highly structured learning environments to ensure a high degree of attention to task. Sessions were organized with students seated at kidney-shaped tables facing their teacher—never with students sitting on floors in the classroom or out in hallways.

Teacher collaboration ensured that parallel block time effectively met the diverse learning needs of all students. Grade-level teams were held accountable for their students' performance. At the beginning of the school year, teachers set SMART goals (Conzemius & O'Neill, 2002) for student performance in core academic areas. For example, the Fox third-grade team analyzed student assessment data and determined that 90 percent of their students would meet or exceed state standards as measured on the state assessment administered in the spring. Throughout the year, building administrators collected results from common formative assessments and posted them for public review in the faculty lounge. This public posting and sharing of data provided the faculty with a constant visual of how far students had come and how far students still needed to move to attain each grade level's SMART goals. While there was variance in achievement growth among grade-level teams, this practice prompted cross-grade-level articulation and exchange of successful teaching strategies. Importantly, these data enabled each team to track their progress and contributed to the strong sense of accountability for results that was beginning to permeate the campus.

Administrators at Fox realized that if grade-level teams were to improve student achievement, team members must be given time to collaborate and discuss the following three questions:

1. Which students are in need of intervention, and which students are in need of enrichment?

2. What will daily lesson plans be for students in both intervention and enrichment blocks?

3. How will we redistribute personnel to deliver this instruction effectively for our students?

Fox administrators discovered that teachers needed blocked time for *planning* as well as for delivery of instruction. Finding additional collaborative time, beyond the parallel block secured for student instruction, required even more dramatic changes to master schedules.

Past scheduling practices at Fox did little to promote collaboration among grade-level teams. Year after year, the preferences of art, music, physical education, and learning center teachers dictated how the master schedule looked and functioned. While a vertical schedule, where a specialist sees one grade level after another, provides specialists with ease in transitioning between periods, it also ensures that grade-level teachers have minimal opportunities to meet and collaborate around the critical questions of learning.

Fox staff created a schedule modeled after the one used by Rebecca DuFour at Boones Mill Elementary School (DuFour & DuFour, 2012; visit **go.solution-tree.com/plcbooks** for a link to a sample schedule) that aligned all specials classes horizontally so all sections of a grade-level team could meet for collaborative planning. By rescheduling in this manner, grade-level teams had two to three hours each week to meet.

Using parallel block scheduling to provide intervention and enrichment has proven extremely effective for systematically allocating differentiated instruction to diverse student learners. Today, every Fox student receives timely, structured intervention or enrichment for 225 minutes per week—all within the course of the 8:40 a.m. to 3:00 p.m. school day. Additionally, increased collaboration helps teacher teams remain focused on the critical questions that direct common planning meetings. Most importantly, student achievement data confirm that Fox is fulfilling its responsibility to ensure that all students master essential skills.

Fairview Elementary School

Fairview Elementary School also provides an excellent case study regarding effective systems of intervention and enrichment. Fairview's approach differed from Fox's but was equally effective in achieving results. As is characteristic throughout District 54, Fairview hosts a diverse student population of 42.8 percent white, 36.3 percent Asian, 14.7 percent Hispanic, 2.6 percent African American, 3.1 percent multiracial, and 0.6 percent American Indian (School District 54, n.d.c). Before PLC transformation, Fairview's assessment results were underwhelming. Prior to the first year of implementation, only 69 percent of students met or exceeded state standards in reading. Achievement data trends dramatically improved after the school initiated new systems of intervention. Within six years, 97.2 percent of Fairview's students met or exceeded state standards in reading.

To prepare for the PLC journey, Fairview's principal and school leadership team began by restructuring the school's master schedule. Realizing teachers' critical need for common planning time, school leaders revamped the master schedule to provide three thirty-minute blocks of common planning time per week. Another concept, "buddy time," provided teams with an additional forty-five minutes per month of collaboration. During buddy time, two separate grade levels paired, and students from one grade level joined their buddy classes to engage in a variety of educational activities. Teachers from one grade level left their students with their buddies and used that time to meet. Participating teams alternated responsibility for supervising buddy activities so that each team could meet once a month.

In addition, Fairview's teachers capitalized on the time available as a result of the district's early student release schedule on Wednesday afternoons. This enabled Fairview's teams to meet regularly and engage in the critical tasks of identifying essential outcomes, writing common assessments, analyzing assessment data, sharing effective teaching strategies, and planning for intervention and enrichment.

After creating opportunities for collaborative planning time, Fairview administrators then focused on developing an intervention structure. Fairview's intervention structure—a three-tiered Response to Intervention (RTI) approach—provides two separate, scheduled blocks for students to receive additional support in areas of need (beyond the Tier 1 regular instruction). In Tier 2 intervention, students participate in three thirty-minute blocks per week. During these blocks, new instruction stops and support staff provide push-in supports to needy students.

Using results from team-created common assessments, teachers regroup students by mastery level of assessed essential outcomes. Students demonstrating mastery on the initial common assessment engage in extension work that is largely independent. Students scoring in the middle range on the initial common assessment receive additional guided and independent practice opportunities on the assessed skills. Students scoring below 80 percent accuracy on the initial common assessment receive teacher-led, focused, small-group instruction that is differentiated to accelerate learning. After five to ten intervention sessions, Fairview's teams issue a second common assessment and analyze results to determine if students in intervention groups have achieved a score of 80 percent or higher on the common assessment. Students not meeting this benchmark continue to work on the assessed essential outcome during small-group or one-on-one instruction.

Fairview also provides selected students with Tier 3 intervention support. Tier 3 intervention involves four additional forty-five-minute sessions per week. Teacher teams use fall and winter MAP assessment results to identify students whose test scores fall below the 40th percentile in the United States. Teacher teams divide these students into groups based on student needs and maintain a teacher-to-student ratio of no more than 1:6. Teacher teams utilize research-based programs as a resource to provide these students with additional support.

Fairview's "Double and Triple Dip" model for intervention has been remarkably effective in improving student achievement results. Equally as impressive, the school has witnessed a significant reduction in the number of students formally identified as "learning disabled." As teachers provided targeted supports in a proactive manner, the number of students with IEPs reduced from forty-three to twelve over a five-year period. Teacher Michelle Thompson describes the impact the intervention system has had on the school community:

> The intervention structure at Fairview is extremely powerful for both the teachers and students. Teachers engage in collaborative conversations to reflect on instruction and plan future lessons centered on common assessments and essential outcomes. As a result of this continuous collaboration between all educators involved, students are retaught or enriched in the strategies, making them proficient readers. Students are excited about intervention time because they participate in meaningful, engaging lessons designed to meet their needs. The results of this individualized instruction are seen in the confidence and attitude of the students as they feel successful and make gains. The students know they are more proficient readers and the teachers know they are more effective educators. (personal communication, August 2010)

Fox and Fairview School developed different systems for providing intervention and enrichment for students, yet each was based on the same premise of reallocating resources and enabling teams to provide additional time to support students in need. Importantly, these interventions were delivered during the school day and provided to all students demonstrating difficulty mastering essential learning outcomes. Both schools saw tremendous achievement gains as a result of their efforts.

Implementing Literacy Intervention: From Individual Schools to District Expectations

During the second year of the PLC journey, teacher teams from Fox and Fairview schools presented their intervention models to administrator and teacher teams from throughout the district. These sessions provided staff members with the opportunity to ask questions and learn from the successes other school teams were experiencing related to PLC transformation. As the district began to examine common practices in schools achieving high degrees of success with their literacy interventions, the district's director of literacy, Erin Knoll, compiled a summation of important structural and instructional considerations that became tight expectations for all schools in the system.

Allocate Time for Daily Literacy Intervention Periods

Intervention periods in all District 54 schools range from thirty to fifty minutes daily in length. Richard Allington (2008) asserts that struggling readers need a minimum of thirty to fifty minutes of daily small-group intervention beyond what is provided during the initial balanced literacy block in order to see measurable gains in achievement. Teachers need to transition students quickly into intervention groups and maximize instructional time during each intervention period to see the greatest impact on student achievement. Teachers need to explicitly teach students to move quickly between classrooms and into different intervention and enrichment groups in order to maximize learning time. Every instructional minute is treated as sacred in a PLC, and time cannot be squandered due to slow transitions.

Assign Support Staff and Resource Teachers to Grade-Level Teams

Support staff—including special education teachers, bilingual resource teachers, and reading specialists—add their support services to grade-level teams during intervention blocks. Additional support allows teams to provide smaller groups for intervention supports. The practice of flooding supporting personnel to assist grade-level teams during intervention blocks reduces the teacher-to-student ratio so that ratios never exceed 1:8. Ideally, this ratio will be even lower for students with the greatest need for precise instruction.

Stagger Literacy Intervention Periods Throughout the School Day

Intervention blocks are staggered throughout the school day to enable resource personnel to flood their support services to different grade-level teams. This mode of scheduling allows special education teachers, bilingual resource teachers, and reading specialists to maximize their contact time with students on their respective caseloads and better support the grade-level teams to which they have been assigned.

Regroup Students Across the Grade-Level Team

The PLC model calls for grade-level teams to share responsibility for ensuring high levels of student learning (DuFour et al., 2008). To this end, grade-level teams at all District 54 schools regroup their students across the grade level during intervention blocks to ensure that teachers with the highest skill for teaching a given strategy or concept work with students each day. Additionally, sharing students across the grade-level team better encourages teams to engage in conversations focused around the critical questions of learning, as all team members share accountability and responsibility for ensuring the success of every student in the grade level. Teams meet regularly to discuss curriculum pacing, common assessment development, assessment administration, and student results. Furthermore, teams collaborate to develop intervention lesson plans that provide each student with extra time and support to achieve essential outcomes.

Create Highly Structured Learning Environments

The classroom environment for students receiving intervention instruction should be highly structured and organized. During intervention, students should not be seated on the floor or taught in hallways or overly crowded classrooms. To ensure attention to task, students receiving intervention instruction should be seated around their teacher at kidney-shaped tables or at desks configured in a half circle, as in the Fox Elementary example.

Administrative Support for Teachers' Efforts

The primary responsibility for creating strong structures to support effective delivery of literacy interventions rests with the building principal. As instructional leaders, building principals must develop master schedules by the first day of each school year that maximize time and support for learning. In schools producing remarkable gains in academic achievement, starting literacy interventions early in the school year has proven to be a critically important variable in closing achievement gaps between proficient and struggling readers and writers (Allington, 2008). Developing master schedules that provide uninterrupted blocks of time for common planning opportunities, core instruction, and intervention periods empowers teachers to provide daily, targeted supports to both struggling and proficient students.

Provide Additional Balanced Literacy Support

Teams should carefully evaluate their instructional plans during intervention periods and prioritize enhancing reading and writing skills. District 54 leaders encouraged teachers to replace low-level skill work and engage students in authentic and rigorous learning activities. Students identified for literacy intervention should participate in daily small-group sessions adhering to a balanced literacy structure. For example, during the forty-five-minute intervention block, District 54 students participate in guided and shared reading and writing as well as vocabulary and word study activities. A typical forty-five-minute intervention might include five minutes of word work, ten to fifteen minutes for shared reading, fifteen to twenty minutes for guided reading, and a writing activity. Adhering to a balanced literacy structure ensures that teachers deliver research-based practices to accelerate learning for struggling students.

Focus on Curriculum Alignment and Coordination

When designing balanced literacy intervention lessons, teachers should focus on addressing the same skills, concepts, and vocabulary that are simultaneously being delivered during initial instruction. In other words, teachers provide students with in-depth exposure to the same content delivered during initial instruction, but in a differentiated, small-group context. Furthermore, teachers should select a different teaching strategy for small-group intervention than was used during initial instruction. Merely replicating the same instructional practice for intervention will likely fail to yield desired results. To determine the skills and areas of focus for literacy intervention lessons, Allington (2008) asserts that the structure of intervention should take its cues directly from initial classroom instruction. The content of literacy intervention lessons should directly align with the skills, strategies, and concepts being addressed during core literacy instruction, a concept referred to as "curricular coordination" (Allington, 2008).

Maximize Time for Authentic Reading and Writing Tasks

As simple as it sounds, the most critical thing teachers can do to improve students' reading and writing skills involves providing regular opportunities for students to engage in authentic reading and writing tasks. As Muir literacy coach Amy Czerniak stresses, "The most important thing a struggling reader can do to improve his or her reading ability is to read every word on every page every time—and do this every day" (personal communication, December 2011).

Use Scripted Intervention Programs as a Resource

While District 54 has purchased many intervention programs to support instruction, these programs only provide students with *additional* support for skills and concepts being addressed during initial literacy instruction. The district discourages the use of canned intervention programs as scripts because students have different learning needs and teaching must be responsive to those needs. As noted previously, prior to PLC implementation, all District 54 schools used instructional assistants to pull struggling students out of literacy blocks, employing canned reading remediation programs that focused on the development of isolated skills to "catch" students up. This approach was a failure across the district and contributed to persistent low levels of achievement over time. Too often students receiving their intervention from scripted programs ended up working on skills, strategies, concepts, and vocabulary that did not align with initial literacy instruction. Focusing on isolated, unrelated skills fragments curriculum and, ultimately, confuses students.

Ensure Maximum Time on Task

Every minute of every school day must be used productively to move struggling students forward. Too often the flow of classroom instruction gets interrupted by behavior distractions, slow transitions, and "filler" work that lacks academic rigor. Intervention needs to be highly structured, crisp, and engaging to students. In a well-designed intervention session, students should be fully attentive to their instructor, who keeps the instructional pace and variety of activities presented filled with energy and variety. Well-designed intervention lessons will provide students with the opportunity to participate in multiple activities including shared reading, guided reading, working with words, vocabulary, and writing to name a few.

Support Teachers' Efforts With Observation and Encouragement

As instructional leaders, building principals and assistant principals should support the considerable efforts of teacher teams to design and deliver powerful literacy interventions. Building administration should devote time each day to observe intervention classrooms and actively monitor the instruction taking place. In so doing, principals and assistant principals can provide timely praise, support, and suggestions to teams that further enhance the learning experiences they provide to students.

Establishing Math Intervention

District 54 focused on establishing and refining literacy interventions during the initial years of its transformation into a PLC because students' reading and writing assessment results lagged significantly behind mathematics; however, the PLC model requires teacher teams to assume collective responsibility for ensuring student mastery of essential learning outcomes in *all* subject and content areas, so the district sought research-based approaches and practices to provide clear direction for math instruction and intervention.

Balanced Math

Under the leadership of the district's director of mathematics, Jim Vreeland, the district developed the tight expectation that all teachers design their math instruction in alignment with the district framework for balanced mathematics. Using the *Everyday Mathematics* series (Bell, 2007), teachers were asked to divide time within each sixty-minute mathematics period as follows:

- Math review (10 minutes)—Students review concepts previously introduced that reinforce computational skills and strategies aligned to the current unit of instruction.

- Shared instruction (20 minutes)—The main focus of the lesson is introduced and modeled by the classroom teacher. Student learning is then monitored, and the classroom teacher targets those students who need additional support or extension with the content introduced during the lesson.

- Guided instruction (two 15-minute rotations each period)—Students receive support based on their current level of understanding based on common assessment data.

The classroom teacher meets with a small group of five to six students to differentiate the content introduced during shared instruction.

- Independent practice (15 minutes)—Students work in small groups to collaboratively complete practice problems, use technology to reinforce skills, or complete problem-solving activities as an extension of the lesson.

This model limits the amount of time spent during initial instruction and requires teachers to break students into small groups each day in order to provide differentiated support for all levels. Strategically scheduling special services and bilingual resource teachers into the guided math portion of math periods further enables teachers to break students into small groups. By having multiple teachers pull small guided-math groups for fifteen-minute chunks of time, intervention time in mathematics is built directly into the structure of the sixty-minute math block.

Guided Math

Laney Sammons (2010) notes in her work *Guided Math: A Framework for Mathematics Instruction* that time should be devoted for differentiated supports in small-group contexts. She notes that during guided math sessions teachers introduce the learning experience, encourage students to identify relevant known skills and understandings, provide time for individual thought, scaffold individual learning, and address learning issues that may arise during the small-group session. Sammons asserts that students benefit from guided math sessions when they are enabled to talk, think, and work their way toward understanding of mathematical concepts, including engaging in conversations with the teacher, making connections, and developing generalizations.

In District 54's prescribed model for balanced math instruction, two fifteen-minute rotations are used during the math block for small groups to work on skills presented during initial instruction and assessed using common assessments. Students failing to demonstrate mastery of material presented during initial instruction or of skills evaluated through common assessment administration are retaught in a small-group format until mastery of the essentials is achieved. As the teacher works with guided math groups to provide intervention supports, the rest of the class engages in independent practice or a variety of workstation activities to further develop numeracy skills. This may involve completing practice problems related to the skill presented during initial instruction, working in groups to complete math journal assignments, or working at computer stations to further strengthen skills by playing mathematics games as part of Everyday Math's online curriculum.

Hoover Math and Science Academy teacher Steven Kyle shares that he has seen tremendous benefits from this model to drive both initial and intervention instruction:

> I strictly follow the district's Balanced Math Framework to organize my math instruction and lesson plans. During Shared Math, I use fill-in-the-blank style notes with many visuals to support our ELL students, as well as a few scaffolded practice questions. I then move into the Guided Math portion to ensure students really interact with the new math concepts and to make sure I am supporting any students who may be struggling with a new or previously introduced skill. During Guided Math, students not working directly with me transition between various hands-on stations. The stations vary between small-group journal work, larger group journal work, Math Boxes, extended response practice, Math Masters (for my high-achieving students), as well as a few online sites that offer interactive practice through skill-based games. Towards the end of the math lesson, I often provide my students with an exit slip or the opportunity to preview their homework. I use this time to assess my students' level of comprehension so that I can gauge who I may need to work with the following day. I am very pleased with what I have been able to accomplish, and I truly believe that the Guided Math system is effective. As a testament to this method, I had a student who entered Hoover in the fall as a struggling math student run up to me to share her excitement over earning an A on a math test! (personal communication, February 2012)

Frost Junior High demonstrated remarkable achievement gains in math by incorporating guided math intervention structures. Former principal Paul Goldberg describes their guided math intervention approach:

> Each day, math teachers met with students in small groups designed to target individual learning needs. Within these groups, students are guided through the content with differentiated material at the appropriate level for student success. Additionally, guided math groups were used to reach students who were not proficient in a particular skill as evident from MAP and common assessment data. Teachers also used this time to conference with students about their progress and help them set learning goals aligned with concepts measured on MAP tests. (personal communication, September 2010)

Frost has seen statistically significant gains in the area of mathematics since implementing this system. Prior to its use, the school saw 92.5 percent of its students meet or exceed math standards as measured by the ISAT. In 2010, 97.4 percent of Frost's students met or exceeded state math standards. Perhaps most impressive is the fact that in 2010, 95.1 percent of Frost's IEP students met or exceeded state math standards—an increase of nearly twenty-six percentage points from two years prior.

Since beginning their PLC transformation in 2005, District 54 leaders have encouraged teacher teams across all twenty-seven school sites to reflect on their successes with developing systems of intervention and enrichment. District and school site leaders have purposefully replicated effective practices from across the system to improve student learning outcomes. Developing highly effective systems of intervention and enrichment involves putting all of the pieces of the PLC process together: Teachers apply essential outcomes to develop common assessments that identify students' specific learning needs. Teacher teams examine assessment results and share responsibility for developing intervention and enrichment supports. This entire process occurs in a collaborative context and, when done well, results in remarkable outcomes for student achievement.

Lessons Learned

1. Focus on Process During Initial Implementation

It has taken District 54 schools time to develop and refine their intervention systems before generating impressive student achievement gains. Common roadblocks during initial implementation included teachers' concern over the time required to plan intervention and enrichment lessons, problems with providing small-group supports given the large number of students in need of intervention, a lack of willingness on the part of some grade-level teachers to share "their" students with teammates for intervention, confusion over who would assume the responsibility for designing lesson plans for different intervention groups, frustration over finding suitable physical locations for intervention and enrichment lessons, and frustration over the loss of instructional time that accompanied regrouping and moving students across classrooms for intervention and enrichment work. There is no quick fix to these issues—districts engaging in this work must simply dive in and address each challenge as it arises.

In District 54, the issue of time faded into the background as teams learned that collaborating and sharing the responsibility and workload actually resulted in saving time once systems were established. The issue of teachers being reluctant to share their students was alleviated by teams learning how to work together and seeing the dramatic achievement results that emerged from the collaborative process. Teachers also took comfort in the realization that the district no longer expected one teacher to meet all of the learning needs of the students assigned to their classroom; instead, teams of teachers would work collaboratively to share their expertise and ownership of the learning experiences for the entire grade level. No one was alone in this work—the collaborative team was all in it together. The more managerial concerns of finding physical space for interventions and managing student movement during intervention periods became less of an issue as teachers and students became accustomed to the new routine. Most importantly, teachers learned that by working together and reallocating time and support in a strategic manner to students in need, there were simply no limits to what students could achieve.

Principals should maintain a tight expectation that intervention and enrichment support be provided every school day. Furthermore, principals should understand that during initial stages of implementation, actual instruction may not be perfect. Principals are encouraged to recognize efforts as teams begin to deliver intervention supports and understand it is challenging work for teachers, particularly if a culture of isolation permeated the school community prior to the PLC transformation. Teacher teams will need ongoing feedback and support as they gain confidence. In time, the quality of instruction will improve and achievement gains will follow.

2. Schedule Interventions as Non-Negotiable

Providing students with additional time and support on specific skills is vitally important to ensure that all students learn and experience measurable academic success. Therefore, schools should have scheduled intervention periods that are not optional—they should be identified in the school's master schedule every day. As DuFour, DuFour, and Eaker (2008) note, students must be required—rather than invited—to devote the extra time and secure the extra support for learning. In addition, because this time is so crucial to the neediest students, it should be considered sacred throughout the school community. Teams should guard against the desire to skip intervention periods (in favor of additional initial instruction, for example), and building administrators should make a point to visit intervention classrooms on a daily basis to observe where and how this critical instruction takes place.

3. Provide Collaborative Planning Time

Designing and delivering powerful systems of intervention and enrichment requires teams to engage in authentic and meaningful collaboration on an ongoing basis. Teacher teams will be constantly engaged in developing and administering common assessments, assigning groups for intervention and enrichment activities, designing differentiated lessons that meet student needs, and evaluating the impact of instruction provided during the intervention and enrichment block. This is intense work, and school leaders must provide teams with adequate planning time to engage in these important tasks. Building administrators should not expect this process to unfold smoothly without providing frequent and uninterrupted opportunities for teams to meet, plan, and reflect.

4. Celebrate Achievement Gains

As collaborative teams commit to providing systematic and timely student interventions, leaders can enhance teacher motivation by validating team efforts and results along the way. Principals may wish to provide teacher teams with recognition for these gains during faculty meetings, all-school assemblies, or through written notes of commendation and praise. In District 54 schools, student achievement gains resulting from the implementation of these systems were shared and celebrated at all school meetings, with PTAs, and simply by having the principals meet with teams to congratulate them on work well done. The district also publicized the achievement gains of schools who were demonstrating considerable growth through stories in newsletters distributed to parents and community members. These types of acknowledgements not only serve to inspire and motivate staff, but they also help foster a healthy and productive school culture.

Conclusion

Designing powerful systems for intervention and enrichment truly involves putting all of the PLC processes together. Teams must work collaboratively to identify essential learning outcomes, develop common assessment measures, analyze data, share effective teaching strategies, and plan a coordinated effort to reallocate time and support to ensure all students demonstrate growth. Importantly, no school is ever "done" with any of this work. Each of District 54's schools have continued to refine their operating practices and processes related to the way intervention and enrichment systems support students. The next chapter will explore ways District 54 has continued to sustain itself as a PLC across each of its school sites.

chapter 7

Sustaining the Process

> *If you waver with your vision, then your staff can and will become unsure of the direction they should be moving. Movement must be forward. All teachers and students must be held accountable for academic growth.*
>
> —PAMELA SAMSON, RETIRED DISTRICT 54 PRINCIPAL

District 54 demonstrated a significant, long-term commitment to becoming a PLC. To achieve this goal, the district strove to make PLC concepts the overriding framework for all decisions—from staffing to scheduling to goal-setting and beyond. Such a deep transformation required the district to provide ongoing training and professional development around PLC concepts, revamp its school improvement planning process to increase accountability for results, restructure district-level supports to reinforce the transformation at individual school sites, and prioritize celebrating achievement gains across the system. Central to the district's success has been the understanding that PLC transformation is an ongoing process—not a one-time event.

Providing Staff Development and Ongoing Training

Providing continued staff development and training is essential to ensuring deep implementation of the PLC model. Too often school districts opt to select PLC training as a focus of professional development for a given school year, only to move on to another initiative for professional development the following year. Because PLC is an all-encompassing framework that addresses all aspects of the way schools are organized and function, staff must receive ongoing professional learning as they continue to refine and develop each key aspect of the model. Additionally, training must be provided to all new hires to ensure they are aware of the culture and operating practices.

New Teacher Training

Orientation to the PLC concept begins immediately for teachers new to District 54. Assistant Superintendent for Human Resources Andy DuRoss introduced the practice of giving a copy of DuFour, DuFour, Eaker, and Karhanek's (2004) *Whatever It Takes: How Professional Learning Communities Respond When Kids Don't Learn* to all new hires when they come to the district office to sign their teaching contracts. All new hires are asked to read this text prior to reporting for new teacher induction week held in early August. On the first day of induction week, the district provides intensive staff development around the core components of the PLC framework. The goal of this opening staff development session is to provide all new teachers with a common vocabulary related to key PLC principles. Furthermore, teachers and administrators from school teams across the district share how PLC is implemented at their school sites so all new teachers know and understand how the district embeds these concepts into daily routines. From the very beginning of a new faculty member's employment in District 54, the district establishes that the PLC is not a fad but rather the overriding framework encompassing all educational work. First-year teacher Sam Natrop shares:

> When I was hired in District 54, I had a cursory knowledge of the function and process of PLC. The day I signed my contract, I received a copy of *Whatever It Takes* and sat down to read it. The success stories were inspiring and captivating. It was clear from day one of our new teacher training that the district was dedicated to the PLC process. Through this process, the bar has been raised not only for students but for teachers as well. I can't imagine teaching without PLC—it has provided me a direction, purpose and support system along with professional collegiality that I've never before experienced. (personal communication, February 2012)

Ongoing PLC Workshops

To provide ongoing support, District 54 has held workshops on PLC implementation for school teams every year since the PLC journey began. These two-day trainings have enabled all staff members to experience direct training. Importantly, members of the board of education, district-level administration, building principals, and assistant principals attend these sessions to learn alongside teachers and provide clarification to school teams when needed. In some cases, school teams participating in these sessions are comprised solely of new hires. In other cases, teacher teams have elected to participate in the two-day training a second or third time to reflect on their progress and determine next steps. Administrators and teachers returning for training have repeatedly stressed its value, as they have been able to focus on different components of the PLC model based on where their schools are now functioning along the PLC implementation continuum.

During each of these training sessions, teams from different District 54 schools have been asked to present alongside PLC experts, such as Richard DuFour and Rebecca DuFour, on the successes and challenges their schools have faced with PLC implementation. This opportunity to take the stage and share effective strategies with other district educators has been extremely rewarding for teachers and has enhanced leadership capacity across the system. Principal Beth Erbach notes that the experience of having her teachers showcase their school's accomplishments was extremely powerful:

> My staff at Fairview had the pleasure of presenting their successful PLC model to the District 54 administrators and representative staff members from each school. This process allowed us to reflect on our practices and procedures along with our achievements. This validated our efforts and accomplishments that we had been developing for the previous three years. The team presentation empowered the staff to internalize all the successes they experienced and to realize the impact they have had on student learning. After the presentation, the staff has been asked on numerous occasions to share their knowledge with schools that are beginning the PLC journey. From the administrative point of view, this caused the school to rally together, work as a team, and motivate all students to reach their highest potential. As of today, Fairview continues to look at its systems and find ways to keep improving and moving children forward as a cohesive staff that focuses on best practice. (personal communication, December 2011)

Mary Kay Prusnick says that these sessions have held particular significance for her as a newly seated board member:

> As a new board member, the best orientation I got to the district's leadership and priorities was PLC training with the DuFours. Going there and hearing their message gave me an excellent explanation of *how* we work in District 54. But the real revelation, for me, came from listening to our school teams present on how PLCs inform student learning and seeing administrators and veteran staff members there working

hand in hand with new hires. All getting the same information at the same time sent a powerful message. It became obvious to me *why* we work this way in District 54—because PLCs help us deliver instruction more effectively to every child. In doing so, we ensure that every child really, truly learns. (personal communication, February 2012)

It is important to note that while many administrators and teachers in the district have been through these two-day trainings multiple times, there is always something new to learn—especially given the unique experiences each school has as the PLC transformation takes shape. Having district and building-level administration attend these trainings has sent a very powerful message to all staff regarding the value the district places on instituting PLC processes.

PLC Audits

At the conclusion of the second year of the PLC journey, Churchill Elementary School volunteered to participate in a structured audit to highlight successes and identify areas for continued growth in their transformation. The audit, facilitated by Tom Many, Rick DuFour, and Becky DuFour, began with members of the Churchill faculty completing an implementation survey regarding specific steps the school had taken to implement a PLC at the site. The audit also required the school to provide practical work products demonstrating how collaborative teams at the school had implemented PLC processes. Among the work products included were samples of team norms, common planning schedules, and common assessments. The audit provided a comprehensive, written narrative summarizing the data and providing the school with substantive feedback related to implementation efforts.

In addition, the audit included a panel discussion with Churchill's School Leadership Team. Leadership teams from other schools in the district attended to learn from the experience. In the course of the panel discussion, Churchill staff members articulated their successes and shared areas they still needed to address so the school could move forward in its PLC journey. The questions posed to the panel included the following:

- To what degree have your grade-level teams clarified the knowledge, skills, and dispositions (essential outcomes) all students must acquire in each course or subject?

- How well do you feel your grade-level teams perform at monitoring each student's learning on a timely basis?

- How effective do you feel your grade-level teams ha[ve] been at providing systematic, timely, and directive interventions when students don't learn?

- How effective are your grade-level teams at developing strategies to enrich and extend the learning for students who are proficient?

- Could your grade-level teams produce the following artifacts?

  + Agreed-upon essential outcomes for your grade level in math and language arts

  + Team-developed curriculum pacing guides

  + Team-developed common assessments

  + An explanation for how your team provides intervention and enrichment instruction

- How does having explicit team norms impact the work of your teams?

- Describe the process for how your teams set SMART goals and how you assess success toward these goals.

- How do your teams deal with obstacles, conflict, accountability, and other kinds of difficult conversations?

- Describe how your teams respond to the critical questions of learning, including the following—

  + Identifying essential learning outcomes

  + Developing common assessments

  + Designing intervention and enrichment activities

- Describe the systems your teams use for organizing, analyzing, and sharing assessment data among teammates throughout the year.

- What does the instruction/assessment/intervention/enrichment cycle look like on your teams?

- How do your teams use the results from common assessments to guide teaching?

- How do your teams ensure that essential knowledge and skills are maintained?

- How are students involved in creating classroom and individual goals and tracking progress toward them?

At the conclusion of the panel discussion, school teams from across the district shared their reactions to Churchill's implementation strategies. School teams also shared successful practices taking place at their respective school sites. Now-retired Churchill principal Craig Gaska comments on how valuable the PLC audit experience was for his school community:

> The audit questions forced us to reflect in ways we otherwise would not have considered. . . . [We later] began the process of re-evaluating our progress and conducting a self-audit using the same criteria. The audit process, in our opinion, is a critical component of the professional learning community process. (Gaska, n.d.)

The district found the PLC audit process to be so powerful in encouraging reflection and refinement of PLC concepts that it has continued to schedule PLC audits for different schools in the system on a yearly basis.

Collaborating Across Districts

During the third year of District 54's PLC journey, the district engaged in a "critical friends" exchange with Kildeer Countryside Community Consolidated School District 96. Under the leadership of Superintendent Tom Many, District 96 had fully embedded PLC practices into their district's daily operations with impressive results. Both districts wanted to bring in an outside perspective to further enhance their implementation of PLC processes. District 54 superintendent Ed Rafferty shared that the cross-district exchange resulted from a sincere desire of both organizations to learn from each other. He notes:

> Schools typically are not good at sharing what works and what does not. Michael Fullan wrote in *Leading in a Culture of Change* (2001), "It is one of life's greatest ironies: schools are in the business of teaching and learning, yet they are terrible at learning from each other. If they ever discover how to do this, their future is assured." We took this idea to heart in our district. As schools found successes and struggles as they embedded the PLC framework into their daily practice, it became apparent that we needed to find the time within the workday for professionals from different schools and districts to meet. . . . Several of our schools developed a "critical friend" relationship with schools in District 96. The formation of these types of professional relationships has been critical to the success of our PLC. (personal communication, October 2010)

During the collaboration, selected District 54 and District 96 schools visited each other to learn more about how each school site incorporated PLC principles into their daily practices. Participants shared their own successes while expanding their repertoire of strategies through exposure to practices effective at other school sites. This process demonstrated the commitment of both districts to extend their learning beyond typical boundaries, and it typifies Fullan's (2001) idea of "lateral capacity building" where cross-district collaboration and articulation lead to growth opportunities for both systems. Both systems benefited from new insights and powerful exchanges of effective practices.

Reflection on Practice: The District 54 Professional Development Symposium

District 54 has continued to seek out new ways for teachers across the district to collaborate and share their successes related to the implementation of PLC practices. In June of 2011, District 54 held its first ever Professional Development Symposium—"A Reflection on Practice." This powerful professional development experience began with a welcome session in which Superintendent Rafferty shared the remarkable achievement gains that had taken place in District 54 since the implementation of the PLC model. Participants then spent the rest of the day attending their choice of over thirty different breakout sessions facilitated by teacher teams representing schools from across the district. Presentations were all related to ways District 54 teachers were utilizing PLC processes, as well as other instructional and cultural strategies, to impact student learning. Sessions were intentionally designed for teachers, by teachers.

The exchange of effective practices from teacher to teacher on display at this event was extremely powerful and opened up channels for further cross-school collaboration. Board member Teresa Huber comments:

> Our Professional Development Symposium was a tremendous benefit to our staff. The hundreds that participated in this event are still raving about it—the excitement, enthusiasm, and admiration for fellow educators was truly palpable in each breakout session. (personal communication, February 2012)

District 54's first Professional Development Symposium—attended by over five hundred staff members—was truly a celebration of the great work happening across the system as a whole. (A program guide from this event is available at **go.solution-tree.com/plcbooks**.) Plans are now in place for the District 54 Professional Development Symposium to become an annual event.

Mentoring and Instructional Coaching

District 54 has placed a high priority on providing job-embedded professional development supports to assist teachers in the work of deeply embedding successful PLC practices. DuFour and Marzano (2011) assert that the best school systems focus their school improvement initiatives on creating conditions to improve the professional practice of educators. One way the district has supported its teachers involves the use of full-time release mentors who, in place of a classroom teaching assignment, work with a caseload of eighteen to twenty-three teachers in their first year in the district. Given the district's widespread commitment to the PLC model, it is essential that new hires understand each of its components and are supported with the implementation of these components. Full-time release mentors establish strong working relationships with the teachers assigned to their respective caseloads by conducting biweekly classroom observations, taking part in debriefing meetings, and coplanning, modeling, and co-teaching lessons. Full-time release mentors provide new teachers with a safe place to ask questions and brainstorm solutions for issues specific to working within the PLC framework. The district's mentor team members have all enjoyed previous successful experiences with the PLC model and share this expertise with new hires.

In addition, district-level instructional coaches have been instrumental in providing teachers with ongoing support. These coaches are centrally based and provide supports to schools working to refine specific components of the PLC framework. Supports are customized to the needs of individual schools and teachers and may include coplanning and modeling lessons, participating in team meetings to analyze student work samples and discuss effective instructional practice, sharing current research, and facilitating buildingwide staff development sessions related to the goals noted in a school's integrated school improvement plan. The coaches have helped teachers improve initial instruction and meeting productivity and maximize the impact of intervention and enrichment sessions. As with the full-time release mentors, members of the instructional coaching team have all had successful previous experiences with a PLC and use the PLC framework to guide their supports for teachers across the district.

Revising School Improvement Planning

As the district continued to evolve in its implementation of PLC concepts and principles, the school improvement planning process changed. Prior to the PLC journey, the district lacked focus regarding how schools analyzed data and developed action steps as part of their school improvement planning process. In truth, the integrated school improvement plans developed by many schools in the system meant little to teachers and held minimal impact on instruction or student learning. These documents were sometimes written by school leadership teams or even simply filled out by the principal. Each fall, principals submitted these documents to the district office where they were filed—never to be looked at again. In reality, the school improvement planning process was designed to meet state-mandated criteria rather than to focus, inform, and motivate staff to enact change for the benefit of students.

Under the leadership of Assistant Superintendent of District Improvement Karen Hindman, District 54 revamped its school improvement planning process. Now the district requires each school to participate in a structured data retreat each fall. Utilizing a model developed by Judy Sargent from the Cooperative Educational Service Agency (CESA) of Green Bay, Wisconsin, school leadership teams work together in a guided process to discover their data patterns, pose hypotheses around their data, and develop school improvement plans that focus their work for the coming year. The goals listed in each school's improvement plan are now identical to the three student achievement goals established by the board of education. This is significant as the entire system now focuses on producing the same achievement outcomes and success is determined using consistent criteria—meeting the following district goals:

1. Students who have attended District 54 schools for at least one year will read at grade level upon entering third grade.

2. Each school will close the achievement gap for all students in reading and math as measured by both district and state assessments.

3. At least 90 percent of all students will meet or exceed standards in reading and math as measured by both district and state assessments.

During the data retreat, grade-level teams examine state assessment data, MAP assessment data, and other in-house common assessment data. Next, the teams set grade-level SMART goals and develop specific action plans that each team will be responsible to complete. Each school leadership team completes a revised integrated school improvement plan template during the data retreat and later presents the plan to staff at each school site for feedback and final consensus. (A sample template completed by the MacArthur Elementary School staff is available at **go.solution-tree .com/plcbooks**.)

The new school improvement process also requires school teams to present their completed school improvement plans to the superintendent and cabinet each fall. Meetings last approximately thirty to forty-five minutes, and each school team discusses the following questions with the superintendent and cabinet:

- How have you organized your staff to provide for collaboration and analysis of student achievement?

- What trends do you see in your school's data, and what are your SMART goals in reading and math?

- How are your subgroups performing?

- What action steps and strategies are your grade-level teams engaging in to improve student achievement in reading and math?

- How are you providing intervention and enrichment supports?

- What is an obstacle you are facing in implementation of your plan and how are you addressing it?

- What support do you need from the central office to achieve your goals for success?

As part of the district's ninety-day school improvement plan review cycle, each January, school teams from elementary feeder schools and corresponding junior high schools meet as a group to share their progress and answer more questions from their colleagues, the superintendent, and cabinet members. This midyear review involves teacher teams presenting their data and action steps by responding to the following questions:

- What do the results of your fall to winter MAP assessment tell you about achievement gains taking place in your school community?

- What percentage of students do you anticipate will demonstrate proficiency on the state assessment in reading and in math?

- Are there areas in the school improvement plan that will be revised to address your current reality?

- What support do you need from the central office to achieve your goals for success?

Teams from each school take great pride in sharing their achievements and successful practices and are honest in reflecting on the areas where growth is still needed in order to attain district goals. Lincoln Prairie Principal Amanda Stochl reflects on the way the district's school improvement planning process has evolved over time:

> We began with the idea that simply completing our school improvement document was enough to improve student achievement. As a result of this practice we were not able to understand how our work was honored or how it impacted our students. The past few rounds of the school improvement process have allowed our staff the opportunity to share aspects of the work we do, as well as to learn from the successes that take place in other schools across our district. Having this platform enables us to ask questions and have cross-school conversations with teachers, specialists, and administrators districtwide. (personal communication, January 2012)

A third and final meeting in the school improvement process occurs in May after the spring MAP assessment has been completed. This meeting operates similarly to the midyear meeting, providing principals with opportunities to reflect on implemented strategies used to improve student achievement. By examining spring MAP results, principals can predict likely success rates on the ISAT and discuss the percentages of students meeting or exceeding growth targets. These meetings again encourage open sharing intended to support principals as they refine systems and practices for improved student learning.

District 54's school improvement planning process has been instrumental in focusing schools across the district on using data to inform instruction and achieve measurable results. The ninety-day review meeting cycle has provided teachers and administrators with the opportunity to openly share their successes and challenges, while learning from each other's experiences along the way. This process also emphasizes a high degree of accountability for school leadership teams and building administration. For principals, job performance evaluations are based on their school's progress toward meeting the board's adopted district goals. In addition, there is a healthy competition that readily comes on display during these meetings as school teams share their results, discuss their challenges and successes, and identify their plans for the future. The district strongly values transparency, including open sharing of data and action plans for success.

Teachers now have great ownership in their building's integrated school improvement plan because they have engaged in a thorough and structured process for reviewing their students' data trends and developing action steps for improvement. Additionally, the central office has learned how to better support schools in their implementation of PLC concepts and principles as a result of listening to administrator and teacher teams explain their successes and challenges.

Restructuring District Supports

As District 54 continued its PLC journey, it recognized the need to ensure that district supports appropriately upheld school-based efforts. One way district leaders improved their support was to limit competing initiatives. By putting all other improvement initiatives on hold, the district clarified their priority of PLC transformation.

Additionally, the district completely restructured the organization of its department of instruction, special education department, and bilingual department. For too long, these departments worked in relative isolation from each other. As PLC practices took hold, building-level administrators noted the need for these departments to communicate and focus their efforts on assisting schools with successful implementation of PLC concepts and principles. Furthermore, as schools transformed into PLCs, staff members began to assume ownership for *all* students' learning. As a result, schools devised new and successful systems of support to meet the needs of English learners and special education students as they engaged in PLC practices. Previously, the district central office mandated the way schools should serve these students. As school teams began to truly take responsibility for the learning of *all* students, these mandates proved to be disruptive to the PLC process. They realized district-level supports needed to be restructured to support a shift in philosophy; grade-level teams, operating within the PLC framework, were in the best position to make instructional decisions to meet the needs of their students, and they needed to be empowered by the district to do so.

To better support schools, in a massive reorganization of district-level supports, the special education department, bilingual department, and department of instruction merged into a single department charged with the task of supporting the PLC initiative. This new department of student learning staff clearly articulated its vision and commitment to supporting the PLC process by drafting the foundational statements shown in figure 7.1.

Vision

The department of student learning is committed to providing service and leadership across District 54 to advance our shared mission of "Ensuring Student Success." We envision the department of student learning as an exemplary one in which we:

- Communicate a common message with openness to new ideas.
- Model the key elements of a professional learning community and do whatever it takes to improve student achievement.
- Provide resources and professional development to support consistent and strategic instructional practices for all students.
- Empower every student to meet or exceed state academic standards.

Collective Commitments

In order to advance our shared vision of an exemplary department, we will:

- Work as a team to make data-driven decisions while capitalizing on individual strengths.
- Care to confront and work to resolve differences through honest communication.
- Work collaboratively to support the needs of individual buildings.
- Communicate in a clear, concise, and timely fashion.

Figure 7.1: Department of student learning foundation statements.

This restructuring proved pivotal in establishing the new norm of focused service and support from District 54's central office to individual schools as they continued on their PLC journeys.

Celebrating Districtwide Success

The District 54 board of education takes great pride in the efforts teachers, support staff, and the administrative team have taken to improve student learning. District 54 has witnessed unprecedented gains in academic achievement since it began implementing PLC practices and principles. To acknowledge this hard work, the board devotes a portion of one board meeting each month to provide public recognition through their Ambassador for Excellence and Above and Beyond award programs. Any staff member can nominate teachers, administrators, support staff, and teams for their outstanding contributions to district performance. Frequently, recipients of these honors are recognized for their outstanding participation in PLC transformation.

Additionally, the board provides formal, public recognition each fall to every school in the system that achieves the goal of having ninety percent of students meet state standards in reading and math. The board hosts a 90/90 celebration at a local banquet hall where faculties from each of the district's 90/90 schools come forward to receive a "90/90 pin" and shake hands with board members to recognize their accomplishments. Healthy competition has emerged across the district as more and more schools have met the district's 90/90 goal. School teams take great pride in being recognized at this annual celebration.

Taking time to celebrate the successes teams and schools experienced on their PLC journeys was important to increasing staff morale and enthusiasm for the PLC concept. District 54 made publically recognizing the significant accomplishments taking place across the system a priority—an important practice given the tremendous time and effort that teachers and administrators devoted to the process of aligning their schools with PLC practices.

Lessons Learned

1. Accept that PLC Transformation is a Long-Term Commitment

PLC is *not* a one-time initiative. Remaining committed while fully implementing PLC concepts and principles requires considerable diligence. District 54 educators understand that a PLC is not an event but rather an overarching framework to guide and focus all district and school improvement processes. It requires long-term commitment. Effective implementation of the model requires educators to engage in an ongoing process of training, staff development, and continual reflection as schools refine and enhance their practices.

2. Embrace Continual Training

Transforming a school into a PLC is a complex and challenging task. This process requires districts to place a priority on continual training to ensure that teacher teams and administrators refine their student support systems and implement best practices to enhance student learning. As new staff members are hired, they need to be trained immediately in PLC processes. Such initial training ensures that new team members possess a sound understanding of the PLC from the very beginning. Additionally, districts should tap into their own success stories and those of neighboring districts to spread effective practices for the benefit of all. The answers to our greatest challenges are often found in our own schools and classrooms. Sharing these success stories can be an effective means to accelerate the transformation process into a PLC.

3. Demand Accountability and Support Success

Schools and districts that hope to become PLCs benefit from establishing systems and protocols that require accountability for results. However, this demand for accountability must be balanced by continual support to teacher teams engaged in the challenging task of becoming a PLC. The integrated school improvement planning process established in District 54 requires schools to meet with the superintendent and cabinet every ninety days. During these meetings, school teams analyze their data and discuss next steps for moving student achievement forward. While the superintendent and cabinet provide suggestions for ways to proceed during these meetings, focus remains more on listening and determining ways the district can provide additional supports.

4. Celebrate Team Successes

Districts and schools engaged in becoming PLCs should understand that there are many pitfalls and challenges associated with overhauling traditional practices and procedures. Change can be frightening and stressful for all involved, even when the change is appropriate and necessary. Districts and schools must place a priority on frequently and publicly recognizing and celebrating emergent successes. When done in an authentic and meaningful way, recognition and celebration validate teachers' efforts and enhance motivation as teams look ahead to their next set of challenges.

Conclusion

Sustaining the PLC process beyond a one-year initiative is key to ensuring deep implementation of the model across a school district. This process requires ongoing training of staff, revising outdated operating practices that inhibit the implementation of PLC principles, and taking time to continually celebrate accomplishments along the way. To delve deeper into the different journeys of District 54 schools related to this important work, the next chapter provides commentary from building principals who successfully facilitated this process at their respective sites.

chapter 8

Administrating Systemic Change

> *We now collectively believe that all students can
> and will learn. We have a common understanding of
> the grade-level outcomes all students are expected
> to achieve, and we work collaboratively to improve
> student learning. The collaborative process has resulted
> in a snowball effect of teachers learning from other
> teachers. There is proof within each of our teams that
> students will achieve at high levels when teachers work
> interdependently to improve student learning. Our
> teams operate in a transparent manner with one goal of
> achieving student success. This focus provides positive
> internal pressure to achieve greater results through a
> collective action orientation.*

—PAUL GOLDBERG, DISTRICT 54 PRINCIPAL

Successful transformation cannot happen without effective leadership from the building principal. Districts seeking to implement PLC concepts at their school sites should know up front that while the central office can provide resources, training, and support, highly passionate and skilled principals are an essential ingredient to successfully transforming schools into high-performing PLCs.

Principals must possess a myriad of leadership skills as they engage in this complex work. Principals of schools functioning as true PLCs must understand the nuances of scheduling, be adept at articulating loose and tight expectations for the faculty, motivate staff through challenging circumstances, maintain effective interpersonal relationships that foster collaboration, and promote a thoughtful vision of their school's future. Understanding the experiences, challenges, successes, and lessons learned from principals who have successfully navigated this process may assist building leaders as they embark on their own PLC journeys. The reflections that follow from District 54 principals speak to the potential impact PLCs can have to effectively transform schools and will help guide leaders as they undertake the transformation in their own schools.

Eisenhower Junior High

Eisenhower Junior High School is one of the most demographically diverse schools in the state of Illinois. The student population at Eisenhower is 34 percent white, 31 percent Hispanic, 17 percent Asian, 13 percent African American, 2 percent Native Hawaiian/Pacific Islander, 2 percent multiracial, and 1 percent American Indian (School District 54, n.d.c). Over one quarter of Eisenhower's students come from low-income backgrounds. Prior to PLC implementation, Eisenhower was a chronically underperforming school. This data reality has completely shifted in the years since PLC implementation.

Before PLC Transformation

Now-retired principal Pamela Samson shares that prior to PLC implementation, "Eisenhower's culture was to settle for whatever the students achieved, and that often wasn't good enough" (P. Samson, personal communication, December 2010). Samson says there was no guiding structure or goal setting to determine how students could achieve more. Eisenhower's test results remained at very low levels. Students, parents, and staff began to believe that was all students could achieve. "After all, look at our feeder schools. What do we expect?" was a common excuse among staff members. Clearly, something needed to change.

At the end of Principal Samson's first year at Eisenhower, the staff attended a two-day volunteer summer retreat. At that time, staff members carefully examined ISAT data and highlighted areas that needed to be addressed both by the entire building and by individual departments. Analysis of the school's demographic subgroup data indicated that ethnic minority groups, LEP students, and students with IEPs were all underperforming significantly in the school—none of these subgroups had more than 45 percent of its students meeting or exceeding state standards in reading or math. The retreat also helped staff begin to build a new culture with an emphasis on working collaboratively toward common goals and supporting one another and Eisenhower students. Samson notes that prior to implementing the PLC process, Eisenhower's teachers worked in isolation and lacked a focus on generating results. Teachers were certainly working hard, but there was an absence of systematic responses to help struggling students or to ensure every student had the skills needed to be successful in school and in life. The retreat was an extremely successful team building opportunity for newly hired and veteran staff. Samson shared that "Finally, everyone had a common goal: *We Can Succeed! We Must Succeed!*"

The Impact of PLC Implementation

Since becoming a PLC, Eisenhower has seen dramatic improvements in achievement data. Eisenhower's students have moved from 77 percent of students meeting or exceeding state standards on all tests combined in 2005 to 93.6 percent of students meeting or exceeding state standards on all tests combined in 2011 (see figure 8.1). In 2010–2011, the school achieved 90/90 status for the first time. Becoming a PLC has been critical in improving the building culture and student achievement. As principal, Samson made sure staff understood that being a high-performing PLC is a school goal and vision. She was determined that staff members understood and supported the strong, student-centered philosophy that the PLC promotes.

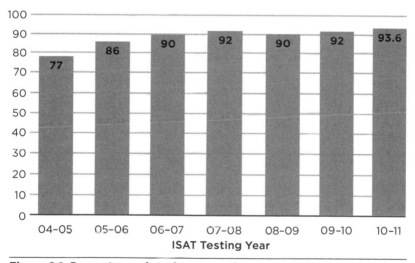

Figure 8.1: Percentage of students meeting or exceeding state standards—all tests combined—for Eisenhower Junior High.

Overcoming Challenges

When Eisenhower began the transformation process, administrators took steps to ensure that the staff understood the need for student improvement. Samson notes that "excuses about why students were not doing better academically needed to stop. Together, the staff needed to believe that strong, resourceful, and consistent daily instruction for all students would lead to improvement" (personal communication, December 2010).

Samson believes the PLC framework fostered a common, universal goal at Eisenhower to "Ensure Student Success!" This new slogan helped set the pace for future building endeavors and eventual successes. The staff formed study groups during Wednesday staff development meetings to discuss the book *Whatever It Takes* (DuFour et al., 2004). This process helped teachers realize that PLC implementation was here to stay.

Samson reflects that Eisenhower staff needed to operate with a focus on common goals, not as individual departments or staff members with different goals: "Staff needed to develop the common belief that all students can learn and that it was their professional responsibility to make sure it happened" (personal communication, December 2010). She recalls a comment shared by a teacher in a faculty meeting during initial PLC implementation: "We needed to change our attitude about our students' abilities. We needed to believe now that all students can be successful learners with the proper guidance, encouragement, and support" (personal communication, December 2010).

Samson shares that one main challenge was encouraging staff to spend more time building solutions to problems rather than falling back on the easy assumption that low achievement scores were the fault of parents and students. She notes:

> Eisenhower staff members needed to decide that they didn't want to be the lowest scoring building in the district anymore. The staff was implementing their own self-fulfilling philosophy. With the negative status of being the lowest achieving junior high in District 54, Eisenhower needed to channel its energy into positive thinking and develop specific and strategic action plans. Staff needed to believe that by working "smarter not harder" they could be successful. (personal communication, December 2010)

She continues, "It would be misleading to suggest that the entire staff was joyous, understanding, and completely on board at the start of Eisenhower's PLC journey; however, once the staff understood that a PLC would improve the school's academic status and benefit students, most got on board." Samson notes that some teachers "sat in the lifeboats" for a while waiting to see if PLC implementation would succeed. These "sitters" never worked against the implementation, but simply waited to see if "this too shall pass." As a building,

Eisenhower succeeded with PLC implementation despite staff uncertainty because Samson and the assistant principal, Kara Prusko (now principal), never stopped sharing building successes, stressing the professional responsibility to ensure student success, and bringing all newly hired staff members on board with PLC training.

Lessons Learned

Former principal Samson provides the following advice for principals to consider as they begin their PLC transformation:

1. Simply go for it, because it works. Be prepared for naysayers, but proceed boldly. Cultivate opportunities for your building teams and departments to collaborate, to work collegially toward common goals, and to believe that all students can succeed.

2. Read and study PLC materials. Take what works for you and your building and jump in. Lead by providing constant support. Provide teams with common planning time. Allow departments and teams to investigate what works for them, and then continue to move them forward. Be prepared to sit with your departments and teams and help them with the obstacles they may encounter. Send your staff members to observe other buildings and classrooms, teams, and departments that have successfully implemented PLC concepts.

3. Move forward. Don't sit back and wait for it to happen. Champion the cause that all students can learn, and remember that is why we became teachers. PLC implementation will not always be easy, but if you truly believe that all students can learn, then this process will help guide your successes. Becoming a PLC will allow you to go home every night and feel that your students have received the very best.

Link Elementary

Link Elementary School provides another example of a building that witnessed strong increases in student achievement data upon implementing the PLC model. Demographically, Link is 56 percent white, 20 percent Asian, 16 percent Hispanic, 4 percent multiracial, 4 percent African American, and 1 percent American Indian and

Native Hawaiian/Pacific Islander (School District 54, n.d.c). The school's LEP population is 16 percent.

Before PLC Transformation

Principal John Schmelzer notes that prior to PLC transformation:

> Teachers collected data, but it served a limited purpose. Teachers examined data because they were told to do so, not because they found it valuable or worthwhile. The staff displayed very little ownership of the data, which varied from grade level to grade level, and there were no universally established data markers used to examine student trends as a whole. (personal communication, December 2010)

In regard to improving student learning, Schmelzer recalls that the culture was very competitive:

> Teachers were judged by student test scores displayed for all to see. This practice was stressful to the staff and discouraged collaboration. It created an atmosphere where just a few teachers felt empowered and the rest felt compelled to do as those teachers dictated, which diminished both innovation and creativity. Teaching became almost prescribed and rote. Many lost sight of the most important thing—the students. (personal communication, December 2010)

Prior to becoming a PLC, Link did not utilize systematic approaches to improve student learning. Schmelzer notes, "Students received reteaching based on their classroom performance, but those opportunities were often inconsistent and informal. If students already received special education support, then they were not eligible for other supports. Thus, support was isolated regarding who intervened and how" (personal communication, December 2010). He asserts that Link had no overriding building approach, only grade-level approaches, to provide student support.

The Impact of PLC Transformation

As a PLC, Schmelzer sees that Link has become a data-driven school where data are meaningful for classroom teachers. Data drive all decisions regarding student learning. Teams look at multiple data points for students and have conversations about student performance. Those conversations include a variety of staff members, not just grade-level teachers or the literacy coach. They include the special services teachers, psychologists, speech pathologists, administrators, literacy coaches, intervention teachers, bilingual teachers, instructional assistants, and grade-level teachers. "The PLC framework provides an umbrella for collaboration that previously was missing. Now when a student is struggling, his or her needs become the collective concern of the entire building, not just an individual teacher or grade level," he says (J. Schmelzer, personal communication, December 2010).

According to Schmelzer, implementing PLC concepts and principles changed the culture at Link immensely. Teachers have internalized the need to collect data and provide interventions and supports for students. Expectations are higher for student learning and achievement because teachers have taken ownership. The PLC no longer represents a principal-driven mandate; it has become a part of Link's daily operation. As noted in figure 8.2, Link's percentage of students meeting or exceeding state academic standards on all tests combined increased from 85 percent in 2005 to 96.5 percent in 2011.

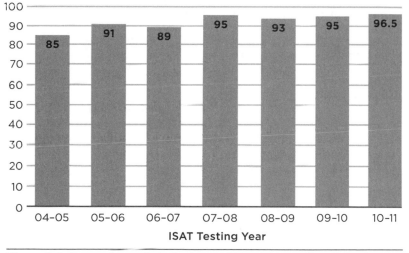

Figure 8.2: Percentage of students meeting or exceeding state standards—all tests combined—at Link Elementary.

Overcoming Challenges

Schmelzer shares that the greatest challenge Link faced involved undoing much of what the staff believed about the PLC concept. He notes, "Before the PLC transformation, teachers collected data with no clear purpose and only inconsistent interventions. Basically, school leaders began the implementation efforts with staff ownership" (personal communication, December 2010). He knew he had to change staff members' mindsets that "PLC" represented just a program or particular time in the day. Instead, staff needed to see the PLC as the guiding philosophy the school would operate under. Therefore, leaders conducted multiple staff trainings on the PLC philosophy and its components. This started with training of the school leadership team and then expanded to training of the entire staff. Principal Schmelzer also met with each individual team to discuss PLC concepts further and provide direct, relevant information. Staff studied successful PLC implementation in other schools and conversed with staff from other buildings to obtain their input.

Another challenge involved finding sufficient time. Link administrators revamped the master schedule to create time for collaboration, interventions, and enrichment. Schmelzer notes, "Teachers had to learn how to collaborate and share ideas. Some teachers struggled to leave old mindsets that there was only one right way to do things" (personal communication, December 2010). By allowing teachers to take risks and supporting them with the resources to be successful, administrators encouraged the rebirth of innovation at Link.

Principal Schmelzer believes that if you were to survey the staff about the PLC versus the "old way" of teaching, no members would desire to change back. In fact, for many, the PLC is all they know. Schmelzer shares:

> When new teachers come to the building, especially those from other districts, they can't believe the support they receive from colleagues. With PLC, teachers experience much more support so that the load is not theirs to carry alone. Teachers' motivation to help all students achieve high levels continues to grow intrinsically; it's not driven by evaluations or the principal. (personal communication, December 2010)

Link's path to becoming a PLC has not been without bumps in the road. They experienced frustrations along the way, including accepting the fact that PLCs are ever evolving:

> What worked one month or for one group of students may not work for the next. Initially, many staff members thought the school would arrive at a point where the schedule, interventions, and staffing would be in place and all would be perfect. No more changes would need to be made. Unfortunately, that is not the case. PLC transformation is very fluid and changes with new students, new staff, and new schedules. Successful transformation requires staff to see that there is never an end. A key is to have good systems in place that are simultaneously systematic yet can adjust to the changes the school may encounter. (J. Schmelzer, personal communication, December 2010)

Lessons Learned

Principal Schmelzer shares the following key lessons for administrators to understand as they begin their transformation:

1. When implemented correctly, PLC holds great power for improving student achievement. According to our experience, the key to implementation is ownership. A PLC cannot be forced on a staff. Success absolutely requires staff buy-in. At the same time, administrators should not provide an option to opt out. PLC implementation requires whole staff commitment.

2. Relationship building serves as an important component when developing a PLC. The principal must establish a culture of trust and respect in the building. Teachers struggle to share data and reflect on their practices if trust isn't established.

3. Implement PLC processes one at a time, and don't get caught up in having everything perfect. The PLC will evolve over time. However, you must eventually have all the components, so persist until the entire framework has been implemented.

4. Principals and staff should visit other schools to witness PLCs in action and talk to those involved.

5. The data speak for themselves. The best part about PLCs is that there are no expensive programs or latest trends to implement. A PLC promotes quality, informed teaching and accountability. A PLC focuses on doing what is best for students.

John Muir Literacy Academy

John Muir Literacy Academy provides another example of how the incorporation of PLC principles and practices have transformed learning experiences for the betterment of students. Muir's diverse demographics include a student population that is 31 percent Hispanic, 21 percent white, 24 percent Asian, 20 percent African American, 3 percent multiracial, and less than 1 percent Native Hawaiian/Pacific Islander and American Indian (School District 54, n.d.c). The school's low income population is 33 percent, and 25 percent of its students are LEP. In spite of these variables, Muir became one of only three schools in the state of Illinois to exit the No Child Left Behind sanction cycle due to the improved academic performance of its students, a direct result of Muir's adoption of the PLC model.

Before PLC Transformation

Former Muir principal Brad Carter shares that prior to the PLC transformation, the reality at Muir was "quite demoralizing." The school has always had a diverse student population and struggled with high mobility:

> Before implementation of PLC concepts and principles, Muir had only 65.4 percent of students meeting or exceeding state standards in reading and 70.4 percent of students meeting or exceeding state standards in math. The school ranked almost dead last in scores within the district. (B. Carter, personal communication, December 2010)

When Carter first took over as principal, Muir was in its second year of not making AYP. This factor enabled families to choose their school of choice within the district. Carter says, "It was easy to blame the school's low performance on having difficult students or simply not enough time with students (because of high mobility), but realistically staff knew they could do better with the right support systems in place" (personal communication, December 2010).

The Impact of PLC Transformation

Carter believes that becoming a PLC has been instrumental to Muir's achievement gains by spreading accountability to all staff rather than isolated classroom teachers. He says,

> Teams share students and provide feedback about best practices to achieve higher gains. While individual teachers might stumble with a group of learners in their class, now teachers have multiple resources (special services, psychologist, literacy specialists, district literacy coaches, administration, and so on) to bounce ideas off of and problem-solve with. (personal communication, December 2010)

Carter shares that prior to the PLC initiative, many Muir teachers felt stranded by classroom needs and overwhelmed. Now the school has a true team approach and all staff share accountability for one another's students. He attributes much of the school's success to their PLC, which helped them develop a laser-like focus on student achievement.

In 2011, Muir saw 81 percent of students meeting or exceeding state standards in reading and 89 percent meeting or exceeding state standards in math. These figures represent a 15 percent increase in reading and 17 percent increase in math over the preceding five years.

In addition, as noted in figure 8.3, Muir moved from having 68 percent of students meeting or exceeding state academic standards on all tests combined in 2005 to 84.9 percent in 2011.

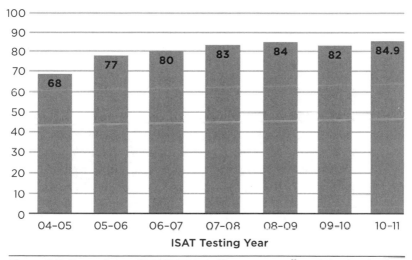

Figure 8.3: Percentage of students meeting or exceeding state standards— all tests combined—at Muir Literacy Academy.

Overcoming Challenges

During the initial stages of the PLC journey, Carter shares that one of the biggest challenges involved creating a schedule that allowed teams enough time to discuss data and address specific student needs. Being a Title I school, Muir had funding available to pay release-time substitutes so teams could meet. The Muir staff also revamped the school's master schedule to enable teams to meet during the school day for common planning sessions.

Carter notes that another challenge Muir faced was the willingness of the staff to accept the PLC framework. He believes that providing everyone with the opportunity to attend PLC trainings created a common language. At first, collaborative teams required many more drop-ins from administration to monitor PLC implementation at each grade level. Today, teams invite administration when needed because they manage their meetings predominantly themselves, focusing on data and best practices.

Lessons Learned

Former principal Brad Carter shares the following key lessons for administrators to understand as they begin their transformation:

1. It is important to revisit your norms regularly as a team. If dysfunction continues unaddressed on a team because norms aren't followed, that aberration will lead to poorer student performance as compared to higher functioning teams. When norms are not maintained, teams begin to not trust each other, and they then experience difficulty in sharing ways to improve student learning. Lost trust can be difficult to regain.

2. Revisit norms every semester and survey teams to evaluate how they are functioning. If issues come up that need to be addressed, a high-performing team takes them on in a collegial way. If a team cannot handle that process alone, then the school administrator needs to step in and provide guidance to clarify expectations.

3. Maintain a collective understanding of the PLC process. Simply sending a small team of teachers to a PLC workshop and then having them return to provide staff development will not ultimately work. Everyone needs to hear the same message and have a clear understanding. PLC serves as the driving force behind what we do at Muir, and I don't ever see that changing. The results prove that it just works!

Jane Addams Junior High

Jane Addams Junior High services a student population that is 51 percent white, 20 percent Hispanic, 15 percent Asian, 8 percent African American, 4 percent multiracial, and 1 percent Native Hawaiian/Pacific Islander and American Indian (School District 54, n.d.c). The school's low-income percentage is 16 percent, and 7 percent of Addams students are of limited English proficiency.

Before PLC Transformation

Principal Steve Pearce shares that prior to implementing the PLC framework, Addams staff worked very hard without seeing the results they desired in student achievement, which affected overall morale. He notes, "Staff members worked in isolation rather than interdependently in teams, and student learning was not necessarily the focus of the entire staff. There were many good things happening at the school, but these good things were not being done in a focused and cohesive manner" (S. Pearce, personal communication, December 2010).

Pearce emphasizes that a great strength of the school was the fact that the Addams faculty genuinely cared about the progress of its students and truly worked hard day in and day out. Yet the absence of effective systems held the school back from reaching the staff's desired goals for student academic performance.

The Impact of PLC Transformation

Pearce shares that since becoming a PLC, Addams has consistent learning and behavioral expectations for all students, regardless of teacher, team, or grade level:

> The staff functions in agreement that the primary school focus is student learning. The lens of learning guides all decision making. Teachers no longer work in isolation; rather, they cooperate in highly collaborative teams focused on essential learning outcomes, quality formative assessment, and targeted interventions. Functioning as a PLC has improved overall student learning at Addams and decreased the number of failing grades issued to students. (personal communication, December 2010)

Pearce now sees that the Addams staff operates with a great sense of urgency to increase student learning, a willingness to do whatever it takes to help students, and high job satisfaction. Staff morale has never been higher. Most importantly, however, student academic achievement levels have soared with the implementation of the PLC. As noted in figure 8.4 (page 116), Addams has moved from having 75 percent of students meeting or exceeding state standards on all tests combined in 2005 to 94.1 percent of students meeting or exceeding standards on all tests combined in 2011.

Overcoming Challenges

Pearce believes the biggest challenge Addams has faced with PLC implementation has been achieving clarity. School leaders spent significant time in Principal Pearce's first year at Addams clarifying what a PLC really is and how it will look in the school setting. Pearce says, "Together, the staff learned about the big ideas of a PLC and what the critical questions really look like in a school. Learning together proved critical to the school's growth as a PLC and represents the biggest influence that changed student learning" (personal communication, December 2010).

Pearce notes that scheduling represents another significant challenge:

> Addams made changes to its master schedule every year to force it to reflect the highest building priorities: providing time for teams and departments to meet and time for students to receive focused intervention and support. Adapting to new schedules has required staff to be creative and flexible. (personal communication, December 2010)

Pearce asserts that the Addams staff has successfully risen to the challenge.

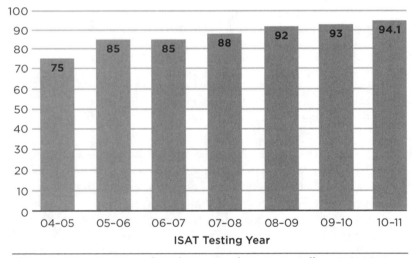

Figure 8.4: Percentage of students meeting or exceeding state standards—all tests combined—for Jane Addams Junior High.

Lessons Learned

Principal Steve Pearce shares the following key lessons for administrators to understand as they begin their transformations:

1. A successful PLC requires leadership, teamwork, and discipline. Leaders must continually go back to the school's mission and ensure that decisions being made support student learning. A good leader will focus on a limited number of objectives and keep going back to them. In a

way, the school has worked hard to simplify the teacher's role by keeping it focused.

2. PLCs do not center on individuals. They require that all staff work together to help students learn, and this collaboration must be reflected in daily attitudes and actions. The goal of a PLC is not to strive to work harder, but to work smarter together as a team.

3. We learned to be disciplined as a staff—to remain focused on the essentials in the classroom. When we have time to collaborate, we stay on the agenda and focus on students. Turning around a school involves hard work and great discipline. However, the positive results make all the effort worthwhile.

Conclusion

Strong principal leadership is an essential element to the successful introduction and cultivation of the PLC process. While each school's journey toward becoming a PLC is different, the lessons are shared by principals who have embarked on the journey and seen its tremendous benefits for students and staff alike. It is important to note an observation shared by Rick DuFour with the District 54 staff during his first visit to the district: no school can truly become a PLC unless the principal is fully committed to the process. This has certainly been the case in District 54. A summation of effective implementation practices follows in the final chapter.

chapter 9

Considering Effective Practices

> *Becoming a PLC has helped create a strong sense of*
> *teamwork throughout the district. Each school is*
> *working toward the same objective and all achievements*
> *are celebrated districtwide. We have consistent voices,*
> *common goals, and are focused on student learning.*
>
> —ED RAFFERTY, DISTRICT 54 SUPERINTENDENT

Schools and districts considering PLC transformation can learn a great deal from District 54's experiences. The district has made a concerted effort to sustain deep implementation of PLC practices, and students have benefited dramatically as a result. Other districts seeking to take a similar journey may benefit from examining the following overall implementation considerations.

Implement With Urgency

A key lesson from District 54's journey involves the district's firm commitment to move with a strong sense of urgency. When beginning the transformation process, administrators used data to confirm the current reality of low student achievement. Instead of bemoaning the challenges inherent in improving student achievement, the district rallied around the PLC framework as a vehicle to dramatically impact student learning and thereby improve students' future opportunities.

The district did not make PLC transformation a five- to seven-year project; instead, the board, administration, teachers, and support staff deliberately engaged PLC practices in substantive and purposeful ways *immediately* following their initial training experience. Missteps certainly have occurred, but these missteps have become learning experiences for schools across the system as each building strives to enhance student support. Importantly, the district placed a strong priority on *action*, rather than deliberating and waiting for 100 percent buy-in to PLC principles and concepts.

Ask the Critical Question

As District 54 rolled out the PLC model, continual dialogue emerged around the critical question "Do we believe *all* children can learn?" (DuFour et al., 2008). In pockets of the district where PLC implementation moved slowly, a key underlying cause was the staff's resistance to change. During initial stages, some teams set low student performance goals, arguing that it was not realistic to expect students from low income, second language, or special education backgrounds to achieve at high levels. As schools across the district began to develop powerful structures of support that generated impressive results with *all* subgroups of children, educators throughout the system came to realize that with the right structures in place, *all* children can experience measurable degrees of academic success. Thus, in those pockets where the framework was not as readily embraced, staff had to consider the difficult question, "Do you really believe all children can learn?" Eventually, throughout District 54, the answer was an emphatic "Yes!" PLC implementation progressed at an accelerated rate and even early doubters of the concept became strong advocates. Confronting this important question proved critical to successful implementation.

Provide Ongoing Training

District 54 sought to intentionally and deeply embed PLC concepts and practices at each of its twenty-seven schools. To ensure this happened, the district focused on continually training new and existing staff and encouraging schools to constantly evaluate their progress along the PLC implementation continuum as defined by DuFour, DuFour, and Eaker. The district avoided moving on to "the next new thing" and instead asked teachers to continually refine their implementation of PLC principles, using data to determine next steps along the way. PLC was not viewed as a one-time training event in District 54. Rather, it has become engrained into the fabric of the district's culture and remains the framework central to all decision making.

Clarify Loose and Tight Expectations

DuFour, DuFour, and Eaker (2008) emphasize the need for leaders to have simultaneous loose and tight leadership—encouraging autonomy and creativity in staff members (loose leadership) within a system of well-defined priorities that must be honored (tight leadership). Clarifying loose and tight expectations during PLC transformation has proved important to District 54's success. For example, the district articulated a tight expectation immediately following the initial PLC training that the district's number one priority would be fully implementing the PLC model across the system. On the other hand, the district was loose in allowing schools to chart out how implementation would unfold at individual school sites, an important variable given the diverse demographic composition, culture, and data reality of each school. As effective practices emerged in the system, district leaders ensured that these practices were shared with all schools, and periodically, new tight expectations were established to replicate successes.

Emphasize Shared Successes and Problem Solving

As individual schools in District 54 experienced successes with implementing PLC concepts, district leaders placed priority on sharing successes throughout the system. In fact, administrative meetings became highly focused around sharing successes, as well as providing time for school leaders to discuss roadblocks. The district has been strategic in asking teaching staff to directly present their successes during staff development sessions on PLC. This exchange of effective practices from teacher to teacher has demonstrated to all staff members in the district that the PLC process works and that the collaborative work of teacher teams accomplishes tremendous achievements. A culture of adult learning permeates the system to an impressive degree. Teacher teams from different schools visit each other to learn more about effective practices and strategies, and principals opened their schools to each other—all done with the goal of improving PLC implementation at each site.

Maintain Communication

District 54 also emphasized clearly communicating its priorities, expectations, and goals for all system employees. Communication represents quite a challenge in a district of twenty-seven schools, but the effort has proved instrumental in moving individual buildings along the PLC journey. It should be noted that the district's union leadership credits the PLC framework with increasing student success, promoting a collaborative spirit among district colleagues, and increasing individual professional development. When asked what the greatest challenges have been for District 54 related to the implementation of PLC concepts, the teachers' union shared the following:

- Scheduling of individual and team planning time for teachers

- Trying to fit all instructional goals into the school day

- Developing common assessments

- Gaining a clear understanding of what each of the district's principals consider to be loose and tight expectations for PLC implementation

To the credit of the district's union leadership, board of education, and administrative leadership, time was taken to problem solve collaboratively and formulate productive solutions around these concerns that are in the best interest of the district's students. Regular meetings between the Schaumburg Education Association executive board and district administrators were held so concerns of members could be openly presented and addressed by the administration. In addition, a Superintendent Communication Council, consisting of the superintendent and two representatives per school, was established in the second year of PLC implementation to provide yet another avenue for communication regarding district goals and operating practices. Building representatives submit any building level questions or concerns from their respective schools, and time is spent openly responding to each item presented.

Make Celebration and Recognition Meaningful

District 54 remains dedicated to celebrating and recognizing the achievement gains that resulted across the system during the PLC transformation. Awarding individual honors, asking teacher teams to present before colleagues, and honoring schools that met the board of education's 90/90 goals all represent ways the district has utilized celebration and recognition of successes to propel PLC implementation forward. There are many challenges that schools and districts face when implementing PLCs, and by recognizing and celebrating successes, staff morale and enthusiasm related to the process remained high and supportive.

Listen to Teachers

District 54's teachers embed collaborative processes into their daily routines and use data to differentiate their instructional practices in order to meet students' needs. In addition, the district's schools continue to refine their support systems and set new, rigorous school improvement goals for the future. As echoed by educators across District 54, teacher Tricia Leong shared:

> I don't know how I would do what I do every day without PLC. Together, our team is able to accomplish so much: we plan our lessons together, create and revise materials, decide how we are going to grade, work through road blocks, share strategies that are working, share our results, celebrate successes, and so on. As a result, we have been able to provide so much more support for all of our students. Not a day goes by where we are not in each others' rooms discussing what we can do next to help our students continue to be successful. PLC has not only enabled us to better help our students but has also made teaching in itself more enjoyable! I love having the opportunity to try new things that our team has created. The PLC model has encouraged teamwork throughout our building and our district. We continue to share strategies and successes with each other as we all have the same end goal: student success. The responsibility no longer falls on one individual. Now, as a team, it is *our* responsibility to help *every* student experience success at school. (personal communication, December 2010)

District 54 teacher Caron Demos shared additional words of inspiration regarding her school's PLC journey:

> PLC has completely changed the dynamics of our school. Since implementation of the concept in 2005, our school's scores have dramatically increased and earned us many awards and recognition. The climate in my school has completely changed for the better—we are unified and positive. The members of our PLC possess a clear vision, have a direct focus, and a unity that is unparalleled. This journey has brought our staff closer than ever before. The PLC philosophy, that once seemed unattainable or just a wish, has become a reality that continues to inspire all of us to work together toward success for all our students and educators. (personal communication, December 2010)

The passion emanating from the words of teachers who have embarked on this journey is remarkable and inspiring. As noted, teachers engaged in the PLC process see the impact their efforts are having on student learning and take tremendous pride in all that is being accomplished as a result of this work.

Ensure Student Success

As a result of PLC implementation, over 2,100 more students in District 54 met state academic standards six years after the district's PLC journey began. This translates to 2,100 more students experiencing measurable degrees of academic success that prepare them for future life success.

Schools and districts embarking on the PLC journey should understand that initial efforts at incorporating the different components of the PLC model will not be perfect. There will be a continual need to return to issues and resolve unanticipated problems. Additionally, each school and district should consider its own context prior to transformation. Schools should possess a clear understanding of their data reality as well as the cultural conditions in place in the school community—these variables will be key in determining where to begin and how to introduce the PLC process to staff members. However, as has been noted with examples from District 54, ample evidence exists that the PLC framework provides the education community with a powerful model to dramatically enhance and improve education and life experiences for students.

District 54 is one case study of just how dramatic the impact of successful PLC transformation can be on improving student learning outcomes for *all* children. Students need different supports, but all students can learn. It is indeed our collective responsibility to revamp support systems and equip our students with the skills and competencies needed to be productive and successful. This work is complex, challenging, and at times, frustrating. However, when educators accept this challenge and fully commit themselves to transforming students' educational experiences, we move closer to fulfilling our shared responsibility of ensuring student success.

references

Ainsworth, L. (2003). *Power standards: Identifying the standards that matter the most*. Denver, CO: Advanced Learning Press.

Abdullah-Welsh, N., Flaherty, J., & Bosma, J. (2009). *Technical report: recommendations for future early childhood literacy research*. Washington, DC: Early Childhood Literacy National Institute for Literacy.

Allington, R. L. (2008). *What really matters in intervention: Research-based designs*. Boston: Pearson.

Axelrod, R. (2002). *Terms of engagement: Changing the way we change organizations*. San Francisco: Berrett-Koehler.

Bell, M. (2007). *Everyday mathematics*. Chicago, IL: SRA/McGraw-Hill.

BIO Classroom. (n.d.). *Bio4Kids: Amelia Earhart (1897–1939)*. Accessed at www.biography.com/assets/pdf/study_guides/bio4kids /Bio4KidsAmeliaEarhart.pdf on October 11, 2011.

Conzemius, A., & O'Neill, J. (2002). *The handbook for SMART school teams*. Bloomington, IN: Solution Tree Press.

Douglas, V. (2003). *Comprehensive curriculum plus test practice, grade 3*. Columbus, OH: School Specialty Children's Publishing.

DuFour, R., & DuFour, R. (2012). *The school leader's guide to professional learning communities at work.*™ Bloomington, IN: Solution Tree Press.

DuFour, R., DuFour, R., & Eaker, R. (2008). *Revisiting professional learning communities at work: New insights for improving schools*. Bloomington, IN: Solution Tree Press.

DuFour, R., DuFour, R., Eaker, R., & Karhanek, G. (2004). *Whatever it takes: How professional learning communities respond when kids don't learn*. Bloomington, IN: Solution Tree Press.

DuFour, R., DuFour, R., & Eaker, R., & Karhanek, G. (2010). *Raising the bar and closing the gap: Whatever it takes*. Bloomington, IN: Solution Tree Press.

DuFour, R., DuFour, R., Eaker, R., & Many, T. (2010). *Professional learning community glossary of key terms and concepts*. Accessed at www .allthingsplc.info/pdf/links/terms.pdf on January 4, 2012.

DuFour, R., & Eaker, R. (1998). *Professional learning communities at work: Best practices for enhancing student achievement*. Bloomington, IN: Solution Tree Press.

DuFour, R., & Marzano, R. (2011). *Leaders of learning: How district, school, and classroom leaders improve student achievement*. Bloomington, IN: Solution Tree Press.

eHow.com. (n.d.). *How to set up a lemonade stand.* Accessed at http://www
.ehow.com/how_107680_set-lemonade-stand.html on February 15,
2012.

Fullan, M. (2001). *Leading in a culture of change.* San Francisco: Jossey-Bass.

Gaska, C. (n.d.). *Winston Churchill Elementary.* Accessed at www.allthingsplc
.info/evidence/winstonchurchill/index.php on January 4, 2012.

Goldberg, P. (n.d.). *Robert Frost Junior High School.* Accessed at www
.allthingsplc.info/evidence/robertfrostjuniorhighschool/index.php
on October 11, 2011.

Hattie, J. (2009). *Visible learning: A synthesis of over 800 meta-analyses relating
to achievement.* New York: Routledge.

Kouzes, J., & Posner, B. (1999). *Encouraging the heart: A leader's guide to
rewarding and recognizing others.* San Francisco: Jossey-Bass.

Marzano, R. J. (2003). *What works in schools: Translating research into action.*
Alexandria, VA: Association for Supervision and Curriculum
Development.

Marx, G. (2006). *Sixteen trends, their profound impact on our future: Implications
for students, education, communities, countries, and the whole of society.*
Alexandria, VA: Educational Research Service.

Neuman, S. B., & Dickinson, D. K. (Eds.). (2001). *Handbook of early literacy
research.* New York: The Guilford Press.

Northwest Evaluation Association. (2012). *MAP© Measures of Academic
Progress TestTaker™ software.* Accessed at www.nwea.org/support
/article/934/map%C2%AE-measures-academic-progress%C2%AE
-testtaker%E2%84%A2-software on February 15, 2012.

Patterson, K., Grenny, J., Maxfield, D., McMillan, R., & Switzler, A. (2008).
Influencer: The power to change anything. New York: McGraw-Hill.

Sammons, L. (2010). *Guided math: A framework for mathematics instruction.*
Huntington Beach, CA: Shell Education.

School District 54. (n.d.a). *Essential outcomes: literacy.* Accessed at http://sd54
.org/literacy/ on February 22, 2012.

School District 54. (n.d.b). *Essential outcomes: mathematics.* Accessed at
http://sd54.org/math/ on February 22, 2012.

School District 54. (n.d.c). *Illinois school report cards.* Accessed at http://sd54
.org/schoolreportcards/ on March 8, 2012.

School District 54. (n.d.d). *Mission, vision, collective commitments, and goals.*
Accessed at http://sd54.org/board/files/2010/04/2007GOALS-with
-2011-12-projects.pdf on February 22, 2012.

index

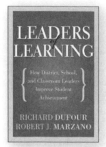

Leaders of Learning
Richard DuFour and Robert J. Marzano
The authors examine how district leadership, principal leadership, team leadership, and effective teachers can improve student achievement.
BKF455

Common Formative Assessment
Kim Bailey and Chris Jakicic
In this conversational guide, the authors offer tools, templates, and protocols to incorporate common formative assessments into the practices of a PLC.
BKF538

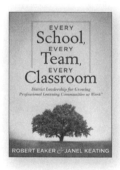

Every School, Every Team, Every Classroom
Robert Eaker and Janel Keating
With a focus on creating simultaneous top-down and bottom-up leadership, the authors show district and school leaders how to grow PLCs by encouraging innovation at every level.
BKF534

A Leader's Companion
Robert Eaker, Rebecca DuFour, and Richard DuFour
Treat yourself to daily moments of reflection with inspirational quotes collected from a decade of work by renowned PLC experts.
BKF227